Self-cater

Spain

PEPITA ARIS

Illustrated by Penny Quested

HarperCollins*Publishers*
New York
London and Glasgow

The Author
Author of *Recipes from a Spanish Village*, Pepita Aris
has had a house in one of the prettiest villages in Andalucia
for almost twenty years. She was editor of the magazines *Good-Cooking*
and *Robert Carrier's Kitchen*, and was founding editor of
Taste. Her husband is a former *Sunday Times*
correspondent for Spain.

Edited and designed by the Book Creation Company Limited,
1 Newburgh Street, London W1V 1LH

Series concept: Jackie Jones
Editors: Eileen Cadman, Sydney Francis
Design: Christine Wood
Index: Hilary Bird
Research: Emma Hurd, David Johnston
Typesetting: Columns, Reading
Printed in Hong Kong

Published by HarperCollins*Publishers*

The Book Creation Company wishes to thank Madeleine Smith for
checking the Spanish.

British Library Cataloguing in Publication Data
Aris, Pepita
Spain. – (Collins self-catering)
1.Spain. Visitors' guides
I. Title
914.60483

ISBN 0-00-436102-4

CONTENTS

CHAPTER ONE
INTRODUCTION   5

CHAPTER TWO
THINKING OF GOING   9
    Region-by-region guide   10
    Accommodation   15
    Rating system   19
    What will it cost?   19
    What will it be like?   20
    What about children and
        babies?   23

CHAPTER THREE
MAKING PLANS   25
    Finding a house or
        apartment   25
    UK-based companies   28
    The travel options   38
    Useful addresses   49

CHAPTER FOUR
GETTING READY   51
    Things to organize   51
    Travel   54
    Holiday money   55
    Taking your car   58
    Holiday health   61
    Useful addresses   62
    At home   63
    What to take   63

CHAPTER FIVE
WELCOME TO SPAIN   66
    Inventory   66
    Things to ask the
        caretaker/agent   71
    Basic shopping straight
        away   73

CHAPTER SIX
EATING AND DRINKING   75
    The Spanish day   75
    Can we drink the water?   76
    Wines, beers and other
        interesting bottles   77
    Eating out   86

CHAPTER SEVEN
GOING SHOPPING FOR
FOOD   99
    The market   99
    The shop   100
    Bread and cake   102
    Groceries   105
    Milk, cheese and eggs   107
    Vegetables   109
    Herbs   111
    Fruit   112
    Poultry and game   114
    Meat and charcuterie   115
    Fish and shellfish   118
    Wine and drinks   124

CHAPTER EIGHT
MENUS AND RECIPES 125
Menus and recipes 126

CHAPTER NINE
CHILDREN AND
BABIES 178
Children's food 178
Eating out 179
Shopping for babies 180
Toilets and nappies 180
Beaches 181
Mosquitoes and ants 183
Cactuses 183
Babysitters 184

CHAPTER TEN
PRACTICAL
HOUSEKEEPING 186
Electricity 186
Butane gas oven 187
Lavatory 187
Rubbish 188
Ants and mosquitoes 188
Laundry 189
Blocked drain 189
Getting help 190

CHAPTER ELEVEN
WHILE YOU'RE IN
SPAIN 193
Survival shopping 193
Local services 195
Health 200
Driving 204
Contact with home 209

CHAPTER TWELVE
EMERGENCIES 212
Emergency telephone 212
Hospital, doctor and
dentist 213
Police 213
Lost property and theft 214
Consular services 215
Insurance 215
Lost credit cards 215
Lost travellers cheques 216

CHAPTER THIRTEEN
BUYING THINGS TO
TAKE HOME 217

INDEX 222

CHAPTER ONE

INTRODUCTION

I have been going on holiday to Spain for almost 20 years. I have shopped there first for tiny children, then teenagers, then cooked for houseparties of adults. Now we have tiny children again as regular visitors. During this period there have been great changes to our Spanish surroundings. New motorways have reduced the time needed to drive across the country. Swimming baths are much commoner, and help with the summer heat. And supermarkets have reached even our village in the south where items from the north, like yoghurt and cream, are now on sale.

Spain is intensely regional, borne out by the use of language. Only around Madrid do they speak textbook Spanish. Everywhere else you will find yourself straining to adapt to a strong regional accent. Something like five languages are current in Spain, the chief ones being Basque and Catalan. From these languages come numerous dialects – in Valencia and Mallorca, for instance, they speak different derivatives of Catalan.

Physically the country is also very varied. The image of Spain that has surmounted all others for the last few years has been of the extended sandy beach, the sun and the orange tree. And this is marvellously true of the main holiday destinations. Spain is, however, a country of mountains and splendid monuments inland, and of rocky coasts and inlets, and of wet weather in the north and north-west. Every part of the country has something to offer the holidaymaker.

Eating well on holiday is part of the fun of being abroad, but even so, the caterer will not want to go to too much bother. You will find that it is far less trouble to do things the local way, because all the ingredients are there to hand. It can be frustrating to miss out on the pleasures of local food, just because you have chosen to eat under your own roof.

Spain differs from Britain much more than do Italy and France, the two countries with which it is most frequently compared. Cookery methods, eating hours, social conventions, the hours that people work, get up and go to bed, are all different. Depopulation of rural areas is also noticeable. Thus Spain still has something that the rest of Europe has almost lost – wild country.

It has taken me some years to get all the varieties of Spanish food sorted out, particularly the fish and *charcuterie*. With this book in hand things will be quicker for you. I hope also it will give you all the tips you need for avoiding annoyance and having the most perfect of holidays.

HOW TO USE THIS BOOK

You'll find that *Self-catering in Spain* is useful at all stages of thinking about your holiday: making plans and organizing; travelling; and once you get there.

The first few chapters will help you during the preparatory stages. Chapter 2 describes self-catering in Spain in a general way. A brief guide to the different regions is followed by a description of the types of self-catering accommodation available, how much they're likely to cost, and what facilities are likely to be (or not be) provided. There's also a special section for those with children. Chapter 3 (MAKING PLANS) covers the various ways of finding a suitable self-catering property, and includes an extensive (but not exhaustive) list of companies that offer self-catering holidays in Spain. The pros and cons of the various travel options are also discussed. Chapter 4 (GETTING READY) lists everything you need to think about when preparing to travel abroad – passports, insurance, currency, health – with useful checklists of items that it's easy to forget.

The book then moves on to what you can expect when you arrive (WELCOME TO SPAIN, Chapter 5). It describes what happens when you take possession of a self-catering property, and includes useful phrases and vocabulary.

Chapter 6 (EATING AND DRINKING) approaches the heart of the self-catering holiday with a description of Spanish habits and customs concerning food and drink. The range of beverages (both alcoholic and non-alcoholic) is described, followed by a trip through the various types of Spanish eatery and what they serve – for the times when you'd rather eat out.

Chapter 7 (SHOPPING FOR FOOD) will give you an excellent start to the adventure of shopping (take this book with you when you go). It provides a detailed description of the shops and markets, and the type of food you'll find in them. The whole range of food is discussed – dairy products, vegetables, meat, fish, groceries, and so on – with tips on how the Spanish cook some of them. Chapter 8 is the core of the book for self-caterers. A wide range of simple menus is suggested (with the shopping list in Spanish alongside), including meals which need almost no preparation and only require a visit to the local shop. Eating like the locals doesn't mean spending hours and hours in the kitchen.

A big worry for some people can be taking children: Will they eat the food? Can you get nappies? How do restaurants react to them? Chapter 9 will reassure you on these points, and provides other practical information about taking children.

The following two chapters – on housekeeping and the practicalities of daily life in Spain – are packed with advice and information on how to keep problems to a minimum, and what to do when things *do* go wrong. Since most self-caterers are likely to have a car, DRIVING in Chapter 11 gives basic information about the Spanish rules of the road and what to do if your car breaks down. Although you're going on holiday to get away from it all, it may be necessary for you to keep in touch with friends or relatives at home. CONTACT WITH HOME, also in Chapter 11, tells you how to make sure that you can be contacted, and how you can contact them if necessary.

While this book strives to be optimistic, it's as well to be prepared in case of emergencies, and Chapter 12 provides brief but necessary practical information about how to cope if one arises. On a happier note, you'll probably want to bring back something to remind you of your trip, and Chapter 13 gives a general description of the enormous variety of things you can buy.

SPEAKING SPANISH

Some people, when planning a trip abroad, rush out and buy the language book and tapes, religiously practise the first three lessons, then put them away and never refer to them again. It's not necessary to do a crash course in Spanish unless you want to. Even on a self-catering holiday, you can get by with the basics. This book includes easy, useful phrases to give you confidence in a variety of situations but apart from these, if you don't have time or energy to do more, all you need to do is learn the courtesies (please, thank-you) and the numbers – it's much more soporific than counting sheep at night. With these committed to memory, you'll be able to understand and make yourself understood (more or less) when shopping – prices, amounts, measurements – and in other practical situations which require knowledge of telephone numbers, or times of planes and trains.

CHAPTER TWO

THINKING OF GOING

Spain is an ideal holiday country for many reasons. It is very beautiful and can offer both sunny beaches and high mountains and an old and interesting culture. Restaurants are cheap, by British standards, outside main cities and the celebrated tourist spots.

The influx of tourists since the beginning of the 1960s has been enormous. In 15 years it jumped from three million to over 34 million, and at the highest point, in 1989, over 50 million foreigners (just under seven million of them British) travelled to Spain in a year. This means that it's easy to find self-catering accommodation near the coast; much of it is let by the travel companies who advertise through the glossy travel brochures. To find suitable property further inland, you will have to look more carefully.

With the influx of strangers came an accommodation of foreign tastes. After all, in summer foreigners outnumber the native population quite substantially in some parts of the country. Discovering that tourists did not always like traditional Spanish food, changes were made to hotels and restaurants. The complaint is now that a diet of pork chops, roast chicken and chips is offered, instead of more interesting food.

The years when Spain was a holiday place where sun, booze and sex were the main attractions are now definitely over. The Spanish are trying to promote a more balanced view of their own way of life. The culture of the country and its scenery and monuments, the traditional ways of doing things, the diversity of the interior and the Spanish cuisine are all coming into fashion with tourists.

Self-catering gives a more intimate contact with the country than you can ever get if you stay in an hotel. There is also the real pleasure of having your own front door, to enter and flop down inside, without hotels and corridor spaces. It is obviously cheaper and more convenient when holidaying with children. They can spread themselves out and be fed at hours that suit them, and you can live *en famille* without bothering about the effect of this on outsiders.

The whole adventure of shopping is a good way of finding out how the locals live, and so experiencing the Spanish way of life to some extent. It will also force you to speak Spanish and is a way to meet ordinary people. Even a little Spanish goes a long way. People appreciate it if you try to speak their language.

REGION-BY-REGION GUIDE

If you are the type of person that likes Scotland and Wales – but feel it politic to try a year away after a disastrous, chilly holiday of rain, then think of the North of Spain. Here the summers are warm, moist and green. It is like a warmer Wales, or like southern Ireland – but with better food.

Galicia, in the far north-west, can be quite blowy, so jerseys are needed in the evenings, although the days are hot. This is the site of Cape Finisterre, so familiar in gale warnings. It also has the Atlantic on two sides, although the sea is a good deal warmer than in the Channel. The city of Santiago de Compostela is a major target for Spanish visitors in the last week of July for the feast of St James the Apostle, Spain's national saint.

Running the whole length of the northern coast are one of the highest ranges of mountains in Europe, the little-known Picos de Europa. Here in Asturias there is much beautiful wild, deserted mountain country. There are bears and chamoix – stout little wild goats with black horns sticking straight up in the air. There are waterfalls and bubbling streams with trout and salmon. This is walking country; I've been snowed on here wearing summer clothes in July. Rural self-catering accommodation is likely to be in scattered farms.

The Cantabrian coast itself, the Costa Verde (green coast) is cut off from the centre by the Picos de Europa. Many Spanish families spend their holidays here. There are lovely beaches in small bays and you are likely to be surrounded by Spanish people, as there are comparatively few foreign visitors here. The accommodation on offer may well be 100 years old, because this area became fashionable as a summer location in the last century. Santander, and San Sebastian further east, are the only places where there is any high-life.

The Basque country, at the west end of the Pyrenees, is small in size, but with its own unique culture. It rains copiously here, except in the summer months, so the landscape is green. The Basques are famed as Spain's restaurateurs, and every sort of produce here, from seafood to beef to vegetables, is wonderful.

The Costa Vasca has high cliffs and fishing villages set in peaceful bays. To the south they have Spain's most famous wine area, the Rioja, although it is rather dull to look at.

South of the Pyrenees is Navarra. Its *fiesta* of San Fermín, with its tradition of bull-running in the streets, was made famous outside Spain by Ernest Hemingway. The Ordesa National Park is spectacular, and best visited in the summer months.

Madrid dominates the plain at the centre of the country. 'Nine months winter and three months hell' is the unkind adage about the capital: *Nueve meses de invierno y tres meses de infierno*. In August the city can indeed be hell to walk in. The *meseta* on which the capital stands is the driest part of Spain, covered with a heat haze in summer. Spring or late autumn are the best times to visit Madrid, as it is cooler, and you can make the most of the city. Madrid sleeps only in the afternoon, and has some of the most sophisticated night-life in Spain. It also makes a centre for touring to other noted landmarks, like Toledo and Avila.

To the south of Madrid lies the flat, dry region of La Mancha – where Don Quixote fought the windmills. The city of Cuenca, in its magnificent location, is well worth a visit. La Mancha is now Spain's largest wine-producing area.

The west of Spain, in Old Castile and Leon, is traditionally one of Spain's poorer areas – and the least accessible from France, if you are travelling that way by car. There are cultural highlights, like the old university city of Salamanca and the cathedral at Guadalupe, home of the famous Black Virgin. Further south, Extremadura has become another of Spain's depopulated areas – an area of scattered villages, holm oaks and pigs. However, the landscape is beautiful. A region for those who really want to get away from it all.

The Costa de la Luz (Coast of Light) is the western, Atlantic coast of Andalucia. It's best known for Europe's largest stretch of wilderness, the Cota de Doñana, now a national park, and the sherry houses at Jerez. The beaches can be windy, although this can be a relief from the sun. Seville, a sophisticated and beautiful Arab city, is known as the 'frying pan of Spain' in summer, when the air is exceptionally still and very, very hot. However, at Easter there are spectacular celebrations, and any type of accommodation is correspondingly scarce and expensive. Tarifa, at the southernmost tip of Spain, is an important wind-surfing centre.

Inland and further east the magnificent city of Granada, like Seville, gives a view of Spain's Arab heritage. There are also the *pueblos blancos*, the white villages in the *sierras*, for those who like a cottage life on holiday. However, once in a hill village, it is difficult to get out without a car. August is really the time to go, for the series of village *ferias* (festivals).

The Mediterranean coast of Andalucia has long been Spain's chief holiday attraction. The Costa del Sol, around Malaga, has the warmest winter temperatures in Europe –

16–17°C in the afternoon at Christmas – pleasantly above 60°F. Remember, though, it has early evenings, and the nights are then cold – and boring. In spring and autumn, however, it offers an escape from the chilly draughts of northern Europe. The area also has the most spectacular Easter celebrations. Book well ahead, if you want to be there for these. The rainy seasons tend to be November and February, and recently these have been of hurricane proportions, with severe flooding. Marbella is the oldest resort on the southern coast, and still the smartest. Torremolinos is another famed beach resort, catering mainly for habitual insomniacs and the fish-and-chip brigade.

Further up the coast, between Almeria and the Cabo de la Nao north of Alicante, are the Costa Almeria, the Costa Calida and the Costa Blanca. There are a number of famous resorts in this area, such as Benidorm, the largest resort on the east coast. La Manga is famous for golf, and prawn cocktails at London prices. Much of the self-catering accommodation in this area is pre-booked by package companies. Inland, in the fertile province of Murcia, the city of the same name was one of the wealthiest during the Arab occupation of Spain.

The coast off Valencia is called the Costa del Azahar, the 'orange blossom coast'. This is Spain's main orange-growing region and the home of the famous *paella*. Charming though it sounds, it seems to be the least popular of all the beach areas. Valencia has a splendid festival in the March *Fallas*. This whole section of the east coast is only easily accessible by air for northerners.

The Costa Dorada (golden coast) is less than golden in places – many of the beaches are polluted, and the main railway line runs along it. Further east is Barcelona, one of the pleasantest cities in Europe (although the traffic pollution can be heavy at times) and a gold-mine for culture-vultures.

Next to the border with France is the Costa Brava, the first cheap beach area to be exploited in Spain and a convenient one, because it can be reached by car across France. The quality of self-catering accommodation can vary considerably. The French are the main visitors. The *brava* of the name means 'wild' and it is a coast of headlands, small bays and villages, rather than the sheets of sand found further to the south.

If you want a cooler place in summer the Pyrenees may suit you. These are serious mountains with secret valleys in between, lying in serrated ranks and forming a border with France. You need a car to get up there. On the Spanish side in Catalonia there are foothills with fruit orchards. For those who like walking holidays, this is a pleasant area to explore, with stiff climbs, pine forests and lots of birds and plant life. In winter there are several famed ski resorts, such as Baqueira-Beret and La Molina, and in summer the passes and roads make driving an adventure. Only 40 years ago, before the tunnel went through, the Val d'Aran was cut off from the outside world for six months of the year by snow, and the mountain peaks around it are still white in midsummer. It is celebrated nowadays for its eateries, as well as for skiing – the Catalans are inventive cooks!

The British popularized the Balearic Isles as they did the Costa del Sol and Valencian coast, and still make up the main summer contingent. The island of Mallorca has long been a popular holiday destination; the sun-lovers inhabit the southern coast around Palma, while the more adventurous explore the wild and mountainous north. Ibiza has been famous as the mecca of the jet-set since the 1960s, but there are still some quiet, rural spots if you look for them. Menorca is more recently developed. The flatness of the island and its comparatively small size – a bus journey across – are against it for some, while for others these facts are merely reassuring. Mahon, the capital, was occupied by the English navy in Nelson's time and there are British features to life there still. Formentera, the smallest of these islands, is worth considering if all you want to do is flop around on the beach.

TYPES OF SELF-CATERING ACCOMMODATION

There is a wide range of holiday lets of various types.

Holiday accommodation was expanded at a great rate in the 1960s, giving rise to terrible stories of tourists arriving at unfinished hotels, and the like. Fortunately, things have changed since then, and now there are more stringent controls on building.

What follows is a general description of the kinds of self-catering accommodation available in Spain. For details of how to find out more and how to book, see Chapter 2, MAKING PLANS.

PURPOSE-BUILT PROPERTIES

Most self-catering accommodation is purpose-built for summer letting, particularly on the Costa Brava round to the Costa del Sol and west to the Costa del Luz on the Atlantic coast. Your neighbours are likely to be other foreign visitors and some of them may well be time-share owners, with a stake in the property. You should check whether, even if the property is 'close to the sea', you have to climb innumerable steps to get to and from the beach.

There are two main types of purpose-built accommodation. The apartment block, built around a communal pool, which will probably be fenced off in some way, with access only through main reception. There are also what the Spanish call *un urbanizacíon*, loosely translated as a housing estate. These are often complete villages of little houses, each with their own front door and a bit of balcony. The Spanish have a great talent for external architecture (little for internal) and these little houses will be in some local style, often with terracotta pantiles, iron balconies and bougainvillaea, and the result is very charming. Sometimes they have their own protected bit of beach – with a guardian on a single entrance to turn away other tourists. They have the feeling of a village when all goes

15

well, but they can be rather isolated if you have no car. You will need transport to get to town or the beach, and might be limited to a single shop built within the complex. The downturn of the tourist market means that there should be a greater choice of self-catering accommodation in beach areas that have been fully booked for the last twenty years.

Flats in *urbanizaciónes* and apartment blocks have been sold to foreigners. About 100,000 Britons now live in Spain, many of whom let out their properties for part of the year through agents and newspapers, to pay off expenses.

PROPERTIES ON THE NORTHERN COAST

Spain's Cantabrian coast is patronized largely by Spanish families. Thus, the demand is stable and so you are unlikely to find something going cheaply. Your neighbours are less likely to be other foreign visitors, and the accommodation may well be more old-fashioned.

VILLAS

These range from the exclusive and expensive – especially on the Costa del Sol and in the Balearic Islands – to something more suitable for those with their eye on the price. Some are designed to accommodate over a dozen people. They usually have swimming pools (shared, in the more moderate price range, with other people) and may be part of a complex containing such facilities as shops and children's play spaces.

FLATS

Most city-dwelling Spanish people live in apartments, although there are now a few houses in dormitory suburbs up the motorways outside Madrid. Spanish flats very frequently have balconies, and the burgeoning plants on them add to their charm. Even the smallest dwelling seems to have some sort of outside patio.

THE *PUEBLOS*

In country places like Galicia, the Pyrenees and Andalucia,

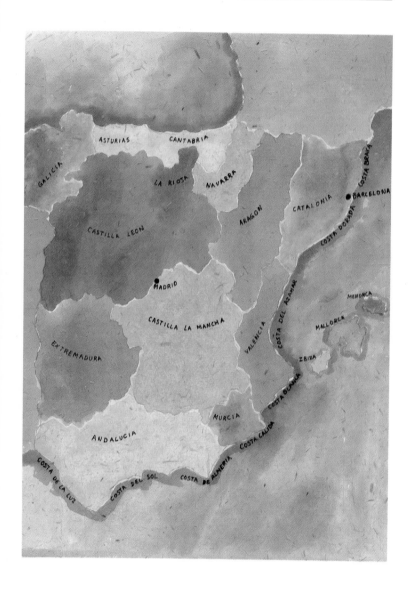

many of the typical little white houses are now being let for the summer. These little dwellings may well be a couple of hundred years old and were previously thought to be unlettable to foreigners. Downstairs they tend to be low and tunnel-like, windows are quaint, and some rooms have none. With the *pueblo blanco* comes a slice of real village life. Your neighbours are likely to be elderly Spaniards, who may be curious about you, and show/give/tell you things that you might find in no other way.

RATING SYSTEM

There is a national rating system for rented apartments, although the requirements it lays down are not very stringent. Equally, your prospective rent may not belong to the scheme – check before you hire.

At the top of the range is the four-key symbol. This guarantees a luxury apartment with air-conditioning in buildings above two storeys, rubbish collection on every floor, private parking, a restaurant or cafeteria in the building (plus your own kitchen), and a reception. Three-key apartments all have reception desks, there are lifts in buildings with more than three floors, and there are telephones in the rooms. Two-key apartments are much as three-key, except that there are no telephones in the rooms, only on each floor. One-key apartments have lifts in buildings of more than four floors, hot water and a shower.

You will have to sign an inventory before you take possession of the apartment. You should check carefully before you sign that everything on the list is in the apartment. (See WELCOME TO SPAIN, Chapter 5.)

WHAT WILL IT COST?

The cost of this sort of holiday in Spain can, like anywhere else, vary enormously. It depends on the location of your house or apartment, on how luxurious it is, and on how you travel. Living costs once you are there should be the same as at home or slightly cheaper, holiday treats excluded.

A real luxury villa with pool can cost from £1800 upwards per week for four people in summer (half that in winter), while a simpler one (still with its own pool) costs around half that amount. A simple purpose-built holiday bungalow or apartment on the coast can be found for something like £200 per week for four in high season – and renovated cottages inland perhaps £250–£300 a week, or even less than £100 per week in winter.

Many holidays include a flight, which tends to bring the average cost for such a package up to around £250 per person for a week's holiday in high season (two weeks work out relatively cheaper). On top of that remember insurance (about £20 each for two weeks), passport renewal, getting to the airport, etc.

By leaving things to the last moment, you can often get a real bargain in self-catering apartments in a coastal development – a 14-day package for £150 is a realistic price.

WHAT WILL IT BE LIKE?

Spain is not a country that prizes domestic comfort highly. Nineteenth-century commentators were always appalled by what they found, even in middle-class homes. It shows in the lack of softening touches – curtains are uncommon in the south, for instance – and also in the basic inconvenient layout of rooms. Reflect that your Spanish agent is probably housed just as uncomfortably as you are.

The main reason is that Spain is a hot country for 10 months of the year in most parts, and people live outside – *viven en la calle*. You will see groups of women sitting outside in the streets on the kitchen chairs in the evening, or family parties of all ages eating out in restaurants or cafes. Social life takes place away from home. Home is just for the chores and a place to sleep, so there is little reason to spend money on making it comfortable.

There is very little air-conditioning in Spain – except in luxury apartments (see under RATING SYSTEM above). Spaniards traditionally go to bed well after midnight – even the children – when it is cooler. Everyone sleeps without any problem in the afternoon – it's so difficult to keep awake! So the need for air-conditioning is less evident.

Another difference is the lighting and attitudes to it. Outside the sun is always blinding. Indoors, Spaniards live a shadowy life. For example, you will notice how badly lit small shops are inside, often with only a single bulb hanging over the counter. The lack of window light is partly to keep the heat down. You will come to be grateful for the shutters over every window in your house or apartment, which exclude the sun very efficiently. Except when rooms are occupied, you should keep the windows shut too. This ensures that rooms stay much cooler than outside. Kitchens and bathrooms rarely have enough light, or in the right places.

As in some other continental countries, beds come with bolsters (covered by rolling the bottom sheet around it) rather than pillows. Take a cushion (and a cover) if you can't bear to be without. Babies sleep in cradles (*una cuna*), and you may well be able to get one, if you ask your letting agent for it in advance. On the other hand, you are unlikely to be able to get a high-sided cot for a two-year-old. The option of bedding the baby in a deep drawer, which works so well in Britain, is probably out too. Spaniards don't keep their possessions in those sort of drawers.

Bathrooms are normally tiled and have a shower and a bidet, so useful for soaking socks and pants at night. Kitchens are usually tiled, and will probably be pretty basic. You are likely to find draining racks for plates but not a great deal else. The oven is almost bound to run on butane gas and these rarely have a regulator – just high and low. Sometimes they have no grills either, since barbecues are universal. The

Spanish stove is much narrower than the models we are used to, so the burners are much closer together. As a result many Spanish cooking pots are tall with narrow bases – like stockpots. There is likely to be some sort of barbecue, as this is such a common way to cook.

Domestic help is common among the Spanish middle-classes so you won't get a dishwasher – they are expensive and a luxury in Spain. A washing machine is also unlikely, although an old-fashioned top loader might be found in some holiday flats. However you should be sure of a fridge with freezer compartment – although it will be fairly small.

Your kitchen cupboard will contain Spanish cooking pots, probably two or three *paella* pans in different sizes for frying. There will be brown earthenware dishes for baking in the oven, called *cazuelas*; you may get oval and round ones, and probably a range of baby ones too. See-through glass (Pyrex) is popular for cups and plates. A traditional Spanish kitchen should have a pestle and mortar, particularly in the south. The chances are that it won't – for this is an item that disappears 'as a souvenir'. Either a mortar or a blender is essential for many Spanish dishes, starting with chilled *gazpacho* soup, and going on to the sauces with pounded nuts that are served with both fish and chicken. Sadly I have omitted these from MENUS AND RECIPES, guessing that you will probably not have the right equipment.

It is a good rule for self-catering holidays always to take your favourite sharp knife, as well as a potato peeler and a corkscrew/bottle opener. You will need a black pepper mill too. Paprika is the principal Spanish pepper, and there are never pepper mills. Matches and candles are a good idea too, since short power-cuts are common.

Local electricity is usually 220 or 225 volts, and a small blender or hairdryer from Britain will work without problems, with a round two-pin plug, or a converter. However, in older properties the supply could still be 125 volts, so check before you go or take dual-voltage appliances if you are booking somewhere classed as 'traditional'.

WHAT ABOUT CHILDREN AND BABIES?

The capacity of young children to sleep almost anywhere, provided they feel safe, makes them easier to take abroad than you might imagine. Stowed into a car, on a plane or train, they may be querulous if it is very hot, or there is a great deal of hanging around, but will usually sleep, waking periodically for drinks.

Heat is the main thing to plan for if you are driving. Sunscreens for car windows are essential – although our family have managed with towels over windows that wind up. On a trip on the straight road from Madrid, for instance, it is possible to drive for four or five hours with the sun in almost the same place, and this can be very uncomfortable for passengers. In the old days, before child seats became the norm, we found that on a trip like this it was preferable to lower the back seat of our Cortina estate, and stack all the luggage on the sunny side. We made the children a nest of bathing towels on the cooler side, where they could lie down.

These days your child will be in a safety seat, and unable to move around. So you will need sunscreens, not only curtains on the back window (with a gap in the middle so that the driver can see out with his rear view mirror) but also side curtains with rubber suction pads. They are available from motoring shops and from branches of Boots. Remember, too, that the metal harness buckles can become quite dangerously hot if the car is left to stand in the sun, so keep the child seat covered with a towel or blanket when you leave the car.

Since wayside loos are only to be found in restaurants, the old standby of a potty in car and packeted baby wipes, with plastic bags for debris, still works. Children also dehydrate easily and it is essential to have water in the car. A large insulated water carrier, with a tap at the bottom and its own cup, is invaluable. I well remember everyone's pleasure when, on the annual drive from Santander to Madrid, we stopped at Somosierra, on the pass over the Guadarrama, and filled up at an ice-cold spring. I have managed with very young children, even sightseeing in summer, by giving them a drink (*un refresco*), or an ice cream every time we passed one. Young children are actually quite tough and sometimes tire less easily than adults. They, at least, are not trying to sight-see and take photographs at same time. They will need long-sleeved clothes and trousers, as a sun shield.

Buying normal provisions for babies should present no problems. Disposable nappies and baby foods are both sold in supermarkets in Spain. The only problems may come if you have hired somewhere in a very small village, or a remote country place. If the item is small, like a pot of nappy-rash cream, take it with you. They are on sale, but the time lost looking for it and the struggle in Spanish is not worth it.

Unless you are going to a purpose-built place that specializes in letting to families, you are unlikely to be able to hire anything in the way of cots or pushchairs. A pushchair, especially for a young baby who spends time strapped into it, must have its own sun umbrella.

The Spanish don't go in for the British straight-sided cot, and only have cradles for very young babies. Spanish children graduate to beds very soon. Nor will there be playpens, because traditionally there have been plenty of brothers and sisters, or a granny, to look after the baby.

On the other hand, you may well think it worth taking the car and all your own equipment. The beaches of the Cantabrian coast or the Costa Brava are only two days' drive across France from a Channel port, while a ship to Santander will land you in Spain itself.

CHAPTER THREE

MAKING PLANS

Obviously, the two most important things to plan are the property and the travelling. These are dealt with in this chapter, which includes a list of travel companies researched especially for this book.

FINDING A HOUSE OR APARTMENT

You may have a property in mind from the outset – one that has been recommended, for instance, or one that belongs to friends. If not, you have to start hunting.

Generally speaking, the earlier you book up the better, as the choice of property for the weeks you want will be better than at short notice. While it's not out of the question, especially in low season, to turn up somewhere and find a house on the spot, this can be a fairly risky plan of action either if children are involved or if the budget won't stretch to a few nights in a hotel, should they prove necessary.

You may start your search in your local travel agency, but a look through the weekend papers will usually reveal a host of small ads. Some are obviously for companies, others describe a specific property and give the owner's phone number (maybe in the UK, maybe in Spain). Some *appear* to be private, but are actually placed by companies.

PRIVATE ADS

There's much to be said for booking direct with the owners – they should certainly know the property and the area, and be able to give quite detailed advice. If it's a house they use regularly themselves, you can be fairly confident that it will be well equipped (and you can ask them, of course – but see also WHAT TO TAKE in Chapter 4).

Theoretically it should be less expensive to book direct with an owner – but you can only know for sure if you make a comparison with properties on offer from the travel firms.

Try to see photographs before you book, and ask for the names and phone numbers of a few 'satisfied customers' – the people you are renting from may *sound* wonderful, but you don't know them, after all.

You will probably be asked for a deposit of something like 25–40% of the total rental. Make sure this is all backed up in writing, and be clear about what happens if you need to cancel. It's usual to get a substantial portion of the deposit back if you cancel a couple of months before planned departure, and to forfeit the whole amount if you cancel at the last minute. Remember that travel insurance will often cover cancellation costs, so look into it as soon as you are about to part with any money. The main thing about booking independently like this is that you have to thrash out these details for yourself.

Properties to be let out to tourists have to be registered with the Spanish authorities as tourist accommodation. Any property you book through a British company should be registered, and the Spanish Tourist Office has a region-by-region list of registered houses and apartments, too. If you make a private booking ensure that you are getting a tourist property – it has implications for insurance and for the use of local facilities (rubbish collection, for instance).

If you book privately, check that the owners have property and contents insurance that covers any damage or breakages you or your party might make, and make sure, too, that their insurance covers you if the roof collapses on one of your party or in case any of you are injured by fire, for instance – unlikely to happen, but it's essential to check.

All of this applies whether the owner is based in Spain, or not. Take into account the cost of international phone calls as you make your arrangements . . .

RENTING FROM FRIENDS

This is likely to be an informal procedure, without any deposits, etc. But check the position on insurance (see PRIVATE ADS, above).

HOME EXCHANGE

Another possibility is house-swopping, which can be arranged through an organization such as Intervac, which aims to promote international friendship. This gives you the opportunity to stay in a genuine Spanish house, while the Spanish spend their holiday in your home. The benefits are many – not least the fact that there is no rental to pay. Contact Intervac Great Britain, Hazel Nayar, 6 Siddals Lane, Allestree, Derby DE3 2DY; phone 0332 558931.

TRAVEL COMPANIES

Broadly speaking, the companies fall into three categories: first, there are the big travel firms who offer countless sorts of holidays to countless destinations, including self-catering holidays in Spain. They often have huge numbers of properties, and these may be handled on site on their behalf by small, local companies. Brochures from these firms are the ones travel agents are most likely to have, and booking can generally be arranged through a travel agent quite easily, as well as direct with the company.

In the middle come the medium-to-large independent operators who specialize in self-catering, with houses and apartments all over the country (and maybe in other countries too), often with 60 or 70 (though possibly several hundred) properties on their books. They tend to resemble either the big firms or the small specialists, depending on the size of their operation.

At the other end of the scale are the independent firms, often quite tiny, specializing in houses in particular regions. A family team with a dozen houses in northern Mallorca or in

Andalucia, say, would be typical. These people are likely to know each house on their list quite well, and might be better than a big company in providing for special requests or needs – if they are given plenty of warning! You generally have to contact these firms direct.

It's impossible to give any hard and fast rules about whether large companies or small ones are likely to be more expensive – our survey of some 65 firms that offer self-catering holidays in Spain showed that the price reflects the location and the luxuriousness of the property rather than company size. Get hold of brochures or information from several firms for the type of property, area and period you want, and make a price comparison yourself.

Most of these companies offer to arrange travel for you. The big firms tend to expect you to arrange your flight through them, so they quote all-in prices. Some companies offer car ferry or motorail as an option, too. Not many offer solely rental. (The specific information on travel comes later, in TRAVEL OPTIONS.)

UK-BASED COMPANIES OFFERING SELF-CATERING HOLIDAYS IN SPAIN

We have tried to make this listing as comprehensive and as accurate as possible, and all the information in it was provided by the companies concerned. Please remember that inclusion in the list does not constitute a recommendation, nor are we suggesting that companies *not* included are unreliable.

As well as names and addresses, the listing includes telephone numbers and, in some cases, special phone numbers for ordering brochures – usually they have an answering machine taking brochure requests, which are dealt with very quickly. The directory also includes the regions of

Spain where the companies operate, plus a short description of their type of business, and the approximate number of properties on their books.

Many of these companies offer travel as well as accommodation – details are provided in the list. Give travel plenty of thought before booking (the options are discussed later in this chapter).

The listing also includes companies' registration with, or membership of, various bodies – ABTA, ATOL and AITO:

What is ABTA? The Association of British Travel Agents is a self-governing body which aims to ensure high standards of service and business practice from its members.

Tour operators and travel agents can be members of ABTA. Members should display their ABTA Number on all brochures and advertising, and are required to adhere to a code of conduct, drawn up in association with the Office of Fair Trading, concerning brochure descriptions, advertising, booking conditions etc.

Should an ABTA member go out of business, the Association will ensure that customers can continue their holiday as planned and return home, and will repay customers who have paid for holidays which have not yet started. In the event of you being dissatisfied with your holiday, ABTA has a conciliation and arbitration procedure for dealing with complaints.

You may therefore prefer to book your holiday through an ABTA travel agent or tour operator for added protection and peace of mind. For further details contact the Association of British Travel Agents (see USEFUL ADDRESSES at the end of this chapter).

What is ATOL? An Air Tours Operators Licence, ATOL, is issued by the Civil Aviation Authority and is a legal requirement for all tour operators who use charter flights (although it does not apply to scheduled flights).

The scheme provides protection for customers such that if the tour company fails, the CAA will ensure that customers on holiday can finish their trip and travel home as planned, and that people who have paid for a holiday which they have not yet taken will be reimbursed. You should look for the operator's ATOL number on brochures and advertisements to ensure that you qualify for this cover. For more information contact the Civil Aviation Authority (see USEFUL ADDRESSES, at the end of this chapter).

What is AITO? The Association of Independent Tour Operators is an alliance of some 70 small tour companies, all specializing in a particular country or type of holiday. All members are fully bonded, either through ABTA, the Civil Aviation Authority, or by private arrangement with insurance companies or banks, so that your holiday is protected.

AA MOTORING HOLIDAYS
P.O. Box 100, Fanum House, Halesowen, West Midlands B63 3BT
Phone 021 550 7401
Fax 021 585 5336
Automobile Association's tour operating branch offering self-drive holidays in Europe for both members and non-members. ABTA ATOL
Approx 100 properties in: Catalonia, Costa Brava.
Ferry Motorail

AIRTOURS
Wavell House, Holcombe Road, Helmshore, Rossendale, Lancashire BB4 4NB
Phone 0706 240033
Fax 0706 212144
Large tour operator offering a wide selection of travel-inclusive, self-catering holidays in Spain and the Balearic Islands. ABTA ATOL
Approx 100 properties in: Costa Brava, Costa Dorada, Costa de Almeria, Costa del Sol, Costa Blanca, Mallorca, Menorca, Ibiza.
Flight Car hire

ALLEGRO HOLIDAYS
15a–17a Church Street, Reigate, Surrey RH2 0AA
Phone 0737 221323
Fax 0737 223590
Small, independent tour operator offering flexible self-catering holidays. ABTA ATOL AITO
Approx 12 properties in: Andalucia, Costa del Sol.
Ferry Flight Car hire Fly/drive

AVON EUROPE LIMITED
Lower Quinton, Stratford-on-Avon, Warwickshire CV37 8SG
Phone 0789 720253
Brochure line 0789 720130
Fax 0789 720982
Family business offering a range of villa holidays for families.
Approx 130 properties in: Catalonia, Costa Brava.
Ferry Car hire Motorail

BEACH VILLAS HOLIDAYS LIMITED
8 Market Passage, Cambridge CB2 3QR
Phone 0223 311113
Fax 0223 313557

Well established tour operator offering a wide range of family holidays in Spain and the Balearic Islands; many of the properties have their own pools. ABTA ATOL

Approx 400 properties in: Costa Brava, Costa del Sol, Costa Blanca, Mallorca, Menorca, Ibiza.

Ferry Flight Car hire Fly/drive Motorail

BLAKES VILLAS
Wroxham, Norwich, Norfolk NR12 8DH
Phone 0603 784141
Brochure line 0533 460606
Fax 0603 782871

Established company offering a range of self-catering holidays in Spain. ABTA ATOL

Approx 32 properties in: Costa Brava, Costa del Sol, Costa Blanca.

Ferry Fly/drive Motorail

CASAS CANTABRICAS
31 Arbury Road, Cambridge CB4 2JB
Phone 0223 328721
Fax 0223 322711

Family business specializing in houses in Cantabria and Galicia.

Approx 80 properties in: Galicia, Asturias, Cantabria.

No travel

CASTAWAYS
2–10 Cross Road, Tadworth, Surrey KT20 5UT
Phone 0737 8122556

Small operator offering self-catering holidays in the quieter regions of Mallorca. ABTA ATOL

Approx 20 properties in: Mallorca.

Flight Car hire Fly/drive

CONTINENTAL VILLAS
Eagle House, 58 Blythe Road, London W14 0HA
Phone 071 371 1313
Fax 071 602 4165

Specialists in villa holidays.

Approx 100 properties in: Costa del Sol, Mallorca, Ibiza.

Ferry Flight Car hire Fly/drive Motorail Train + car hire

CV TRAVEL
43 Cadogan Street, London SW3 2PR
Phone 071 581 0851
Brochure line 071 589 0132
Fax 071 584 5229

Family business specializing in self-catering properties in the quieter areas of Mallorca. ABTA ATOL AITO

Properties in: Mallorca.

Flight Car hire Fly/drive

EUROPEAN VILLAS
154–156 Victoria Road, Cambridge CB4 3DZ
Phone 0223 314220
Fax 0223 314423

Small family business offering travel-inclusive, or rental only, self-catering holidays in the less developed areas of Spain. Accommodation is in detached villas with private pools. ABTA ATOL AITO

Approx 200 properties in: Costa Blanca, Ibiza.

Ferry Flight Car hire Motorail

FALCON LEISURE GROUP
Astley House, 33 Notting Hill Gate, London W11 35Q
Phone 071 757 5555
Fax 071 727 0497

This division of a large company specializes in self-catering apartments. ABTA ATOL

Properties in: Costa Brava, Costa Dorada, Costa del Sol, Costa Blanca, Mallorca, Menorca, Ibiza.

Flight Car hire

GORDON OVERLAND
76 Croft Road, Carlisle, Cumbria CA3 9AG
Phone 0228 26795
Fax 0228 26795

Travel consultancy specializing in villa rental.

Approx 20 properties in: Navarra, Catalonia, Andalucia, Barcelona, Costa Brava, Costa del Sol.

Ferry Flight Car hire

HARTLAND HOLIDAYS
Brunswick House, 91 Brunswick
Cresent, London N11 1EE
Phone 081 368 9595
Fax 081 368 0148

Small company specializing in
self-catering and fly-drive holidays.
ABTA ATOL

Properties in: Galicia, Asturias,
Cantabria, Basque Country,
Castilla–Leon, Navarra, La Rioja,
Aragon, Castilla–La Mancha, Catalonia,
Extremadura, Murcia, Andalucia,
Valencia, Madrid, Barcelona, Seville,
Costa Brava, Costa de Almeria, Costa de
la Luz, Costa del Sol, Mallorca,
Menorca, Ibiza.
Ferry Flight Car hire Fly/drive

HORIZON HOLIDAYS
4 Broadway, Edgbaston Five Ways,
Birmingham B15 1BB
Phone 021 643 2727
Fax 021 643 7267

Large tour operator specializing in
travel-inclusive villa and apartment
holidays in scenic locations. ABTA
ATOL

Properties in: Costa de Almeria, Costa
del Sol, Mallorca, Menorca, Ibiza.
Flight Car hire

HOVERSPEED LIMITED
International Hoverport, Marine
Parade, Dover, Kent CT17 9TG
Phone 0304 240101
Brochure line 0304 240202
Fax 0304 240099

Tour operator branch of the ferry
company.
Properties in: Costa Brava.
Ferry Car hire

INTASUN HOLIDAYS
Intasun House, Cromwell Avenue,
Bromley, Kent BR2 9AQ
Phone 081 290 0511
Fax 081 466 4406

Major tour operator offering a range of
travel-inclusive, self-catering holidays
throughout Europe. ABTA ATOL
Properties in: Costa Brava, Costa

Dorada, Costa de Almeria, Costa del
Sol, Mallorca, Menorca, Ibiza.
Flight Car hire Fly/drive

INTERHOME LIMITED
383 Richmond Road, Twickenham,
Surrey TW1 2EF
Phone 081 891 1294
Fax 081 891 5331

Large accommodation agency offering
chalet, villa and apartment holidays.

Properties in: Valencia, Barcelona,
Costa Brava, Costa Dorada, Costa del
Azahar, Costa de Almeria, Costa de la
Luz, Costa del Sol, Costa Blanca,
Mallorca, Menorca, Ibiza.
Ferry Motorail

INTERNATIONAL CHAPTERS
102 St John's Wood Terrace, London
NW8 6PL
Phone 071 722 9560
Fax 071 722 9140

Privately owned tour company
specializing in top end of the market,
self-catering properties. ABTA AITO
Properties in: Ibiza.
Ferry Flight Car hire Fly/drive Motorail

JEAN HARPER HOLIDAYS
20 Walton Road, Stockton Heath,
Cheshire WA4 6NL
Phone 0925 64234
Brochure line 0925 68778
Fax 0925 602021

Small company specializing in villas and
apartments in Mijas and Menorca.
ATOL

Approx 25 properties in: Costa del Sol,
Menorca.
Flight Car hire

LANCASTER HOLIDAYS
26 Elmfield Road, Bromley, Kent
BR2 9AQ
Phone 081 290 0511
Brochure line 0274 736644

Large tour operator offering a range of
self-catering holidays in Spain. ABTA
ATOL

Properties in: Costa Brava, Costa
Dorada, Costa del Sol, Costa Blanca,

Mallorca, Menorca, Ibiza.
Flight Car hire Train + car hire

MAZARRON VILLAS
18 Wheatfield Drive, Ramsey,
Huntingdon, Cambridgeshire PE17 1SH
Phone 0487 710337
Fax 0487 710 323
Specialists in privately owned villas,
some with pools, in Puerto de
Mazarron.
Approx 75 properties in: Murcia, Costa
Calida.
Flight Car hire

MENCO LIMITED
20 Walton Road, Stockton Heath,
Cheshire WA4 6NL
Phone 0925 64234
Brochure line 0925 68778
Fax 0925 602021
Family business offering luxury villas
and apartments with pools. ATOL
Approx 30 properties in: Madrid,
Menorca.
Flight Car hire

MEON VILLA HOLIDAYS
Meon House, College Street,
Petersfield, Hampshire GU32 3JN
Phone 0730 66561
Fax 0730 68482
Medium-sized company specializing in
private villa holidays with inclusive car
hire. ABTA ATOL
Approx 180 properties in: Costa Brava,
Costa del Sol, Costa Blanca, Mallorca,
Menorca, Ibiza.
Ferry Flight Car hire

NEW CENTURY HOLIDAYS
LIMITED
Cathedral House, Wilkes Walk, Truro,
Cornwall TR1 2UF
Phone 0872 72367
Fax 0872 223776
Medium-sized self-catering specialists
offering accommodation ranging from
basic village houses to luxury villas in
unspoilt areas. ABTA ATOL
Approx 200 properties in: Asturias,
Andalucia, Seville, La Alpujarra,

Granada, Costa de Almeria.
Ferry Flight Car hire Fly/drive

OSL
4 Broadway, Edgbaston Five Ways,
Birmingham B15 1BB
Phone 021 643 2727
Brochure line 021 632 6282
Fax 021 643 7267
Medium-sized company offering villas,
apartments and farm-houses, mostly
with private pools. Car hire is included
in the price of every holiday. ABTA
Approx 55 properties in: Mallorca,
Menorca, Ibiza.
Flight Car hire

PALM INTERNATIONAL TRAVEL
COMPANY LIMITED
Willowdene, Victoria Road, Heaton,
Bolton, Lancashire BL1 5AT
Phone 0204 849029
Fax 0204 849040
Family business specializing in luxury
villas with pools.
Approx 17 properties in: Catalonia,
Costa Brava.
Ferry Flight Car hire Fly/drive Motorail
Train + car hire

PALMER AND PARKER HOLIDAYS
63 Grosvenor Street, London W1X 0AJ
Phone 071 493 5725
Brochure line 049 481 5411
Fax 071 408 1580
Specialist tour operator dealing with the
top end of the villa holiday market.
ABTA ATOL AITO
Approx 50 properties in: Costa del Sol.
Ferry Flight Car hire Fly/drive

PALOMA HOLIDAYS LIMITED
6 Farncombe Road, Worthing, Sussex
BN11 2BE
Phone 0903 820710
Fax 0903 823008
Privately owned, independent company
offering a range of villas with pools in
Spain. ABTA ATOL AITO
Approx 45 properties in: Costa Blanca,
Menorca.
Flight Car hire

PRIVATE VILLAS LIMITED
52 High Street, Henley-in-Arden,
Solihull, West Midlands B95 5AN
Phone 0564 794011
Fax 0564 793494

Company producing a full-colour
magazine featuring privately owned
villas and apartments throughout Spain.
Bookings are made directly with the
owner.

Approx 1000 properties in: Catalonia,
Murcia, Andalucia, Valencia, Costa
Brava, Costa Dorada, Costa del Azahar,
Costa Calida, Costa de Almeria, Costa
del Sol, Costa Blanca, Mallorca,
Menorca, Ibiza.

Ferry Flight Car hire

REDWING HOLDINGS PLC
Groundstar House, London Road,
Crawley, West Sussex
Phone 0293 519151
Brochure line 0293 540207
Fax 0293 23828

Part of a major tour operator offering
self-catering apartments throughout
Europe. ABTA ATOL AITO

Properties in: Costa Brava, Costa
Blanca, Mallorca, Menorca, Ibiza.

Flight Car hire

SAGA HOLIDAYS LIMITED
The Saga Building, Middelburg Square,
Folkestone, Kent CT20 1AZ
Phone 0303 857000
Brochure line 0800 300456
Fax 0303 48622

Large tour operator specializing in
holidays for over-60s. ABTA ATOL

Approx 4 properties in: Costa del Sol.

Flight

SECRET SPAIN
Model Farm, Rattlesden, Bury St
Edmunds, Suffolk IP30 0SY
Phone 0449 737664
Fax 0449 737850

Small family business specializing in
self-catering holidays to unspoilt areas of
Spain.

Approx 75 properties in: Galicia,
Asturias, La Rioja, Costa Verde.

Ferry Fly/drive Motorail

SELECT HOLIDAYS
Centurion House, Bircherley Street,
Hertford SG14 1BH
Phone 0992 554144
Fax 0992 552458

Medium-sized tour operator offering
self-catering holidays in Mallorca and
Menorca. ABTA ATOL

Approx 50 properties in: Mallorca,
Menorca.

Flight Car hire

SFV HOLIDAYS LIMITED
Summer House, Hernes Road,
Summertown, Oxford OX2 7PU
Phone 0865 57738
Brochure line 0865 311331
Fax 0865 310682

Large tour operator offering a wide
selection of villa holidays in Spain.
ATOL

Properties in: Valencia, Costa Brava,
Costa Blanca.

Ferry Flight Car hire Fly/drive Motorail
Train + car hire

SKYTOURS HOLIDAYS
Greater London House, Hampstead
Road, London NW1 7SD
Phone 081 200 8733
Fax 071 357 8451

Large tour operator offering a range of
self-catering holidays in Spain. ABTA
ATOL

Approx 25 properties in: Costa Brava,
Costa de Almeria, Costa Blanca,
Mallorca, Menorca, Ibiza.

Flight Car hire

SPANISH HARBOUR HOLIDAYS
16 Upper Oldfield Park, Bath BA2 3JZ
Phone 0275 823759
Fax 0225 499845

Small company offering apartments and
villas, many with pools, in the less
commercialized areas of the Costa
Brava.

Approx 85 properties in: Costa Brava.

Ferry Flight Car hire Motorail

TAILORMADE HOLIDAYS
2 Cally Hall, Blackshawhead, Hebden
Bridge, West Yorkshire HX7 7JP
Phone 0422 842680

Small company offering a range of self-
catering holidays in Spain.

Approx 10 properties in: Andalucia,
Valencia, Costa Brava, Costa de
Almeria, Costa del Sol, Menorca.

Ferry Flight Car hire Fly/drive

TARLETON TRAVEL AGENTS
LIMITED
Tarleton House, Tean, Stoke on Trent
ST10 4LG
Phone 0538 722231
Fax 0538 723040

Family business offering flights and
holidays to the Costa de Almeria. ATOL

Approx 20 properties in: Costa de
Almeria.

Flight Car hire Fly/drive

THE MAGIC OF SPAIN
227 Shepherds Bush Road, London
W6 7AS
Phone 081 748 7575
Brochure line 081 748 4659
Fax 081 563 0480

Specialist company offering villas (some
with pools) and apartments in scenic
and unspoilt areas of Spain. ABTA
ATOL AITO

Approx 120 properties in: Asturias,
Costa de la Luz, Costa del Sol,
Mallorca.

Ferry Car hire Fly/drive

THE TRAVEL CLUB OF
UPMINSTER
Station Road, Upminster, Essex
RM14 2TT
Phone 04022 25000
Fax 04022 29678

Established, direct-sell tour operator
offering travel-inclusive holidays to
northern Mallorca and Menorca. ABTA
ATOL

Properties in: Mallorca, Menorca.

Flight

TJAEREBORG LIMITED
194 Campden Hill Road, London
W8 7TH
Phone 071 727 2680
Brochure line 071 727 7710
Fax 071 229 3808

Large, direct-sell tour operator offering
accommodation in self-catering
apartments and bungalows. ATOL

Approx 32 properties in: Costa del Sol,
Mallorca, Menorca, Costa Blanca.

Flight Car hire Fly/drive

TRAVELLERS' WAY LIMITED
Hewell Lane, Tardebigge, Bromsgrove,
Worcestershire B60 1LP
Phone 0527 36791
Fax 0527 36159

Family business specializing in
renovated cottages in Andalucia and
unspoilt coastal areas.

Approx 30 properties in: Andalucia,
Costa de la Luz, Costa del Sol.

Car hire

VILLA SELECT LIMITED
Pool House, Coughton, Alcester,
Warwickshire B49 5HX
Phone 0789 764909
Fax 0789 400355

Specialists in rental of luxury villas with
pools to the independent traveller.

Approx 68 properties in: Mallorca,
Menorca.

Flight Car hire

WINTERSUN LIMITED
Unit 2, Boleness Road, Wisbech,
Cambridgeshire PE13 ZRB
Phone 0945 588862
Fax 0945 64991

Small business offering 'try before you
buy' rentals for newly retired people
considering living in Spain.

Approx 9 properties in: Costa de
Almeria.

Ferry Flight Car hire

THE TRAVEL OPTIONS

Travelling to Spain from the UK, the main options are:
fly/drive (i.e. with a hire car waiting at your destination); *flight only*; *taking your car* – using ferry or hovercraft and driving through France, or ferry to Santander on Spain's northern coast; *taking your car and using motorail* (including a ferry crossing); *train* (with ferry crossing); going by ferry without a car to Santander, then train.

As you decide how you want to travel, weigh up comfort/speed/stress etc. against cost. The main points to take into consideration are:

- whether you want to treat the journey as part of the holiday or as a necessary evil
- how much holiday you have and how long you are prepared to spend travelling
- how far you live from the main ferry ports, and how far into Spain your destination lies
- how far you live from an airport
- how far you are prepared to drive
- the number of people who can share driving
- the timing: if you're thinking of driving through France, remember that the French roads are packed on the first and last weekends of August, and during the weekend of their 15 August public holiday
- whether you want/can afford to make overnight stops
- the size of the party (a full carload costs much the same to transport as a half-empty one)
- whether your party minds long sea crossings or flying
- how unrestricted you want your luggage to be (i.e. do you need a carload of baby things, or the windsurfer?)
- whether you can afford the expense of transporting your own car

TAKING YOUR CAR – DISTANCE, ROUTE AND ATTITUDE

If you decide to drive, there are two approaches you can take – the dawdler or a dasher. Dawdlers make the journey a part of the holiday, acknowledging that there's plenty to see en route to or from their main holiday place. Dashers pile into the car and *drive*. It's quite common for members of a party to have differing attitudes to the drive, some being by nature dawdlers, while others are dashers, so compromises often have to be made. You could always dash one way and dawdle the other.

If you live in the Midlands or South, it's quite straight-forward and quick to get to a Channel port and hop over to France. Crossings from the south-east corner of England (Dover, Ramsgate, etc.) are plentiful and fast (details of ferries appear below). From the West Country there are much longer Channel crossings that deposit you in Brittany; from Plymouth you can take the ferry all the way to Santander on Spain's northern coast. Travellers from South Wales can get down to the West Country ports fairly easily.

From the North, North Wales or Scotland there's a long and exhausting drive to the Channel ports, before the drive on the other side of the Channel even starts. And while the prospect of a long drive may not sound too bad when there's a two-week holiday in which to get over it, think of the return journey . . . back late on Sunday and back to the old routine next day, probably.

Whether your destination in Spain is the north-west (past Santander) or the east coast (the Costa Brava), the most direct route is to skirt round the western side of Paris. The *Entre Deux Mers* toll autoroute sweeps across France and runs almost parallel with the Pyrenees, offering many convenient stopping-off points for Spain. If you are coming from a westerly Channel port the French motorways on this side of the country are excellent (and free) and you may join it well south of Paris.

Dashing through France, you will inevitably use the *autoroutes*. Most of France's motorways are toll roads (*autoroutes à péage*). Prices per kilometre vary, and travelling from, for example, Calais to the Pyrenees will cost around £30. This will be in addition to the cost of petrol. (Prices are per vehicle, irrespective of the number of passengers.) Spanish roads with an A prefix are toll routes, too.

Until the opening of the motorway, the drive from Madrid in the centre to Barcelona on the east coast took nine hours. Going flat out, on good roads, it still takes two days to cross the country from north to south, if you go through Madrid. And that's not counting the stretch through France.

MOTORAIL

The idea of Motorail is that you and your car make a substantial part of your journey by train. British Rail offer the service within Britain, while French Railways (SNCF) offer a Motorail service to the south from some channel ports and Paris. The only through Motorail service likely to help the traveller to Spain is the Calais–Narbonne service. This is a night train, with a connection with the lunch-time crossing from Dover. It then travels on to Boulogne, to pick up cars and passengers there. The train arrives in Narbonne about 11.00 the next morning. From Narbonne there is easy access to the Costa Brava and the toll road along the Mediterranean coast south as far as Alicante. The cost for a medium-size car (long cars are quite a bit more expensive) in summer with two adults and two children is about £600 if you hire *couchettes*.

A more expensive option, but one that saves another whole day on the journey, is to take Motorail right down into Spain – the *Puerta del Sol* train. This service is run by RENFE, Spanish Railways, and operates from Paris, so you will probably decide to motor to there. The service departs from Paris in the evening and arrives in Madrid at around 11.00 next morning. Bookings for this train are only accepted 2 months before the date of travel. The cost, for the same family (in couchettes) is approaching £800. Breakfast is provided on arrival at your destination while your car is being unloaded; the train also has a restaurant car and is air-conditioned. This train has another advantage – French and Spanish railways have different rail gauges. At the border, passengers usually have to get out with their luggage and transfer to another train. On this train, though, the *couchette* cars are moved bodily onto the new rolling stock while their passengers slumber inside.

Good Motorail services run within Spain, all of them passing through Madrid. It is possible to cross the border then pick up a train at Irún (at the eastern end of the Pyrenees) to take you further south or west.

Motorail journeys are timed to take place overnight. No conventional accommodation is provided, so you pay for either a *couchette* or a sleeper compartment (*wagon-lits*). A *couchette* is a berth in a compartment – usually there are six people (in triple bunks that fold up to provide seating by day) in each, and you are supplied with a blanket and fresh linen.

You may find that the firm you book your house through will arrange Motorail for you (see the list of companies). Motorail through France (and the *Puerta del Sol* train) can be booked through French Railways in London. Motorail can also be booked through P&O European Ferries and through Sealink (see USEFUL ADDRESSES at the end of this chapter).

FERRY SERVICES

FERRY SHIPS

For a long crossing or a short one, ships can be good fun on hot summer days when the decks are pleasant to sit out on or stroll around. Inside, the facilities and catering seem to vary enormously not only from one shipping line to another, but from ship to ship. In summer, the cheapest channel crossing a family of four with a car can make (travelling at inconvenient times) is around £100.

The port you depart from, and the time of day you cross,

may well be determined by where you live in Britain. Though the short channel crossings are cheapest, Dieppe will get you further on your way south. If you cross in the afternoon and make an overnight stop in northern France, you should reach the Spanish border at the end of the next day. If you cross overnight to a Brittany port you still have the chance of getting through France in a single day.

Facilities on board vary according to the length of the voyage, but there's always food, some sort of duty-free shop, and money-changing facilities. Sometimes there are telephones. TV lounges are quite common, and on longer journeys you may find there's a small cinema on board. Some areas are no smoking.

A single ferry goes direct to Spain: from Plymouth to Santander on the North coast. It leaves England at breakfast time on Mondays, and at about midday on Wednesdays, which permits driving there from further afield. The sailing takes 24 hours. The cost for four plus car, assuming a 4-berth cabin with its own shower and WC is around £600. Of course, you could travel for considerably less as foot passengers. The ship has facilities like disco and cinema to ease the strain of packing and getting away.

Not all the ferries are ships, of course:

HOVERCRAFT

On several of the short routes (such as Dover–Calais) hovercraft cross the Channel in about 40–45 minutes. They carry cars, as well as passengers. They tend to be fairly noisy and to vibrate quite a lot – and even if you get a window seat the view is usually obliterated by spray. However, they halve the journey time (although you take just as long over check-in and customs clearance as in a ferry ship). Refreshments are usually offered (payment required) and a selection of duty-free goods is brought round.

SEACAT

These Australian vessels were introduced by Hoverspeed in summer 1990. They are rather exciting high-speed ferries that cut the crossing time from Portsmouth to Cherbourg by nearly half. They take cars.

The list below shows the ferry routes, the companies and the journey times. Actual departure times are not included as they vary from season to season. [S] Summer sailings only, [C] Seacat. Hovercraft are operated by Hoverspeed.

For further information contact the ferry companies (see USEFUL ADDRESSES at the end of this chapter).

From	To	Company	Duration (hours.min)
TO SPAIN			
Plymouth	Santander	Brittany Ferries	24
TO FRANCE			
Cork	Roscoff	Brittany Ferries	15
Dover	Boulogne	Hoverspeed	.45
Dover	Boulogne	P&O European Ferries	1.40
Dover	Calais	Hoverspeed	.45
Dover	Calais	P&O European Ferries	1.15
Dover	Calais	Sealink	1.30
Folkestone	Boulogne	Sealink	1.50
Newhaven	Dieppe	Sealink	4
Ramsgate	Dunkirk	Sally Lines	2.30
Rosslare	Cherbourg	Irish Ferries	17
Rosslare	Le Havre	Irish Ferries	23
Plymouth	Roscoff	Brittany Ferries	7
Poole	Cherbourg	Brittany Ferries	4.15 [S]
Portsmouth	Caen	Brittany Ferries	6
Portsmouth	Cherbourg	P&O European Ferries	4.45 [S]

Portsmouth	Cherbourg	Hoverspeed	2.40 [C]
Portsmouth	Le Havre	P&O European Ferries	5.45
Portsmouth	St Malo	Brittany Ferries	9

Depending on your starting point and destination, these may be useful, too:

TO BELGIUM

Felixstowe	Zeebrugge	P&O European Ferries	5.45
Hull	Zeebrugge	North Sea Ferries	14.30

TO HOLLAND

Hull	Rotterdam	North Sea Ferries	14
Sheerness	Vlissingen	Olau Line	8

TRAIN

If you are not taking a car and do not like flying, train travel could provide a good solution – but an expensive one. You could hire a car to use at your destination (see HIRING A CAR, this chapter). Although you could go all the way by train if you wish, there's no reason why you shouldn't drive or take the train to Plymouth, cross to Santander as foot passengers, and use a train at the other end. Likewise you could drive to any Channel port, cross as foot passengers and then take the train from the French Channel port, possibly picking up a hire car at the station at the end of your rail journey.

This sort of arrangement might need careful planning to make sure it worked financially, as a return train trip from London to the Costas via Dover–Calais and France is around £150 per adult. (There are reductions for children and young people, depending on their age.)

Though long-distance rail travel through France is now extremely fast, thanks to their high-speed TGV (*trains à grande vitesse*) network, the international trains are not TGV. You would have to make several changes and pay extra to use the TGV, which would hardly be worthwhile.

The main disadvantage about relying on the train to get to your destination is that most of the trains from Calais to Spain stop at the border, and *you have to change* – even in the middle of the night, and often even if you have a couchette. So when finding out details of trains make sure you get precise information about what happens at the border.

Some tour companies (see the listing) arrange rail travel or rail travel and car hire. But it's very easy to arrange this yourself. British Rail International (Victoria Station, London – see USEFUL ADDRESSES) can arrange ferry or hovercraft plus train to anywhere in Spain, starting either in London or at a port. They also have a credit card booking service, so you can book and pay for international tickets over the phone and simply pick them up on your way. Your own railway station may be able to advise.

While Spain doesn't have a high-speed train like the TGV, its fastest and most comfortable train is the air-conditioned *Talgo*. (See LOCAL SERVICES in Chapter 11.)

FLIGHTS

Although normal tickets on scheduled flights (allowing you to change departure dates and times after booking) are expensive, there are much better deals available if you book well in advance, or spend at least one Saturday night away, or plan to be away for at least a month. (In each of these cases you have to fix dates and times when you book, and they cannot be changed later.) Airlines such as British Airways or Iberia are the obvious ones to ask, but you might find that a less well known operator offers flights from your local airport to one close to your destination. You can ask a travel agent or simply ring the airport. Flights can be booked through an agent or direct with the airline. You can sometimes do it over the phone if you have a credit card.

The other sort of flights are the charters, and Spain is one of the biggest charter destinations. At their simplest, they work as follows: big tour companies charter a plane able to take, say, 150 passengers from Birmingham to Malaga each Saturday through the summer, and to bring 150 back. However, it could be the case that they end up with less than 150 holidaymakers, so they sell flight-only deals to independent travellers to fill up the seats. Travel agents can usually find out about this and make bookings for you.

As a very rough guide, a standard air fare to a Spanish city might cost about £180 return; a non-transferable one booked in advance may be £95 or so; while a charter could be anything from £65 upwards.

Scheduled flights do have some advantages: they seem to fare better than charters on those busy summer days when air traffic congestion causes hold-ups. They may depart and arrive at more sociable hours than charters. Remember that a 4 a.m. departure might mean a night in a hotel, or a special taxi ride – balance that against the possible extra expense of a scheduled flight.

Very cheap deals can sometimes be found in the back of the Sunday newspapers, from travel agents who sell tickets bought in bulk. While these may be tempting, it is advisable to check the details fully before sending any money, although they are probably quite above board.

It is very risky to rely on getting cheap, last-minute, flights if you have already booked your accommodation for specific dates.

Travelling by air, you always have to pay for children, and usually for even quite tiny ones. However, this varies from airline to airline, so do check. Get an assurance, too, that the child gets a seat and does not have to sit on your lap. People with babies in carrycots are usually put in the seats with plenty of leg-room – but do ask. And find out whether you can make a seat reservation as you book – this varies from airline to airline, too, and can depend on the type of ticket you have. Generally speaking, the assistance and facilities are better when planes are not too crowded, and worse on a full flight.

Baggage is restricted on planes. It's usually 20kg (about 40lbs) which is more than most people can carry comfortably.

If you are worried about exceeding your allowance you're probably packing too much. Uncrowded flights are much less strict about allowances than full ones.

Take into account the hidden costs and the total journey time: investigate the practicalities of a 5.30 a.m. departure before you pay for it. Watch out, too, for the departure time at the other end – will you need a night in a hotel on your way back? It's worth looking into the expense of railway, taxi or car-parking. Don't ever park in the airport short-stay car park unless you're just dropping people off or picking them up – a fortnight in there would cost almost as much as your holiday. As far as time goes, although the flight itself may be a mere hour and a half, add up the time getting from home to the airport, hanging round at the airport, etc.

HIRING A CAR

If you wish to hire a car for your holiday it is a good idea to arrange this from home before you go as this is likely to be considerably cheaper than arranging it upon arrival. You can also be more sure about the terms and conditions of the rental agreement.

You may find that the company through which you book your accommodation also offers car hire. Alternatively, the large car-hire companies, as well as many other travel agents and tour operators, offer car hire abroad. It is advisable to shop around for the best deal as many of these firms offer special deals for holidaymakers inclusive of local tax and insurance.

Be sure to specify special needs, such as child seats, when you arrange the hire, rather than when you arrive at your destination.

If you do decide to arrange to hire a car when you get there, things are a bit more complicated. Check the terms of the rental very carefully. If it is not based on unlimited mileage, make sure that the car's current mileage is recorded on the booking form. You should also ensure that any damage to the vehicle is recorded, that you are fully insured, and that the car contains all the necessary equipment (see TAKING YOUR CAR – THE PRACTICALITIES in Chapter 4).

MOUNTAIN PASSES

The main entry points for Spain are at the eastern end of the Pyrenees (Irún), and at the western end (Port Bou). At both of these the motorway sweeps across the border. However, you might prefer the historic Roncevalles Pass, with a dramatic climb and views of the mountains. The minor crossings through the Pyrenees often involve high driving, with some tight, unguarded bends (caravans and trailers are sometimes prohibited).

Check details of passes you will use (Michelin maps are useful). Smaller ones may close at night, and many only open from mid June to September. Tolls are sometimes payable. More details are available from tourist offices or the AA/RAC.

TUNNELS

An alternative to passes on some mountain ranges are tunnels. Again, it's best to check the details of tunnels you might use when you plan your route. They vary in length, some being as long as 15 kilometres (9 miles). The quality can vary, too – some are beautifully lit motorway-style tunnels, while others (such as the Viella tunnel in the Pyrenees) are still rough-hewn from the rock with dodgy lighting. Tolls may be payable, and vary considerably.

Be careful to note any special driving regulations concerning, for example, speed limits and the use of sidelights. And if you're driving by day, remember to turn on your lights as you enter and turn them off after you emerge! If you're wearing light-sensitive sunglasses, they can take some time to adjust to the rapid change of light.

USEFUL ADDRESSES

Name	Address	Phone
Association of British Travel Agents	55–57 Newman Street London W1	071 637 2444
Automobile Association	Fanum House Basingstoke Hampshire RG21 2EA	0256 20123
British Airways	Heathrow Airport TW6 2JA	081 759 5511
British Consul (Madrid)	British Embassy Calle de Fernando el Santo 16 Madrid 4	091 419-02-00
British Motorcyclists Federation	Jack Wiley House 129 Seaforth Avenue Motspur Park Surrey KT3 6JU	081 942 7914
British Rail International	Victoria Station London SW1V 1JY	071 834 2345
Brittany Ferries	Reservations Offices The Brittany Centre Wharf Road Portsmouth PL1 3EW	0705 827701
Civil Aviation Authority	ATOL Section CAA House 45–59 Kingsway London WC2B 6TE	071 832 5620
French Railways (SNCF)	179 Piccadilly London W1	071 409 3518

Iberia International Airlines of Spain	130 Regent Street London W1R	071 437 5622
Irish Ferries Limited	2–4 Miriam Row Dublin 2 Ireland	0001 610511
North Sea Ferries	King George Dock Hedon Road Hull North Humberside HU9 5QA	0482 795141
Olau Line Limited	Sheerness Kent ME12 1SN	0795 580010
P&O European Ferries	Dover Kent ME12 1SN	0304 203388
Royal Automobile Club	130 St Albans Road Watford WD2 4AH	0923 33543
Royal Yachting Association	RYA House Romsey Road Eastleigh Hampshire SO5 4YA	0703 629962
Sally Ferries	The Argyll Centre York Street Ramsgate Kent CT11 9DS	0843 595522
Sealink UK Limited	Travel Centre Victoria Station London SW1V 1JT	071 828 1940
Spanish Embassy	24 Belgrave Square London SW1X 8QA	071 235 5555
Spanish National Tourist Office	57 St James's Street London SW1A 1LD	071 499 0901
Thomas Cook Travel	5–7 Priestgate House Priestgate Peterborough PE1 1JF	081 889 7777

CHAPTER FOUR

GETTING READY

THINGS TO ORGANIZE

PASSPORTS

Check that passports are valid for the duration of your holiday. Once they are 16, children need their own passport; before then they can be included on one or both parents' passports (on both is best, just in case one of you needs to come home urgently, for instance).

The standard, 10-year passport, valid worldwide, costs £15. You can obtain application forms from main post offices; the form has to be countersigned by someone who has known you for two years. You need two photographs, as well. You send it to your nearest passport office. *Arrange passports early* - they can take ages, especially during the summer months.

A British Visitor's Passport costs £7.50. It is only valid for one year, so is an expensive option. Also, it is only valid for travel in western Europe (this may have been revised by the time you read this).

INSURANCE

You are strongly advised to take out travel insurance before you go abroad. Holiday insurance will generally cover the following: loss or damage to baggage, loss of money, personal liability, personal accident, departure delay, cancellation or curtailment, legal expenses and medical expenses (including return home in an emergency).

A particularly useful feature of some policies is a 24-hour English-speaking helpline which can be contacted to organize emergency assistance for you.

If you're using a credit card to pay for your holiday you may be able to benefit from free travel insurance, which is now offered by some credit and charge card companies. (Check with the company.)

If you book your self-catering accommodation through a UK company, they will probably offer travel insurance. Otherwise it can easily be arranged through travel agents, ferry companies, banks, motoring organizations and insurance brokers and costs around £20 per person for a two-week holiday (with a 50% reduction for children). You can usually organize it on the spot.

Whatever the policy, make sure that it is adequate – at least £100,000 of medical cover in Europe, plus related expenses such as emergency dental treatment, ambulances and if necessary the cost of returning to the UK. Look out for exclusion clauses. For instance, some policies will not cover you if you are driving, pregnant or over 70 years of age; and check whether the clause about 'pre-existing illness or defects' might apply to you. If you're planning to go hang-gliding, rock climbing or motorcycle riding check that you'll still be covered in the event of an accident.

Remember that in almost all cases where medical treatment is concerned, you will have to pay up front and reclaim costs from the insurance company. The same goes for car repairs, or any other expenses, so keep all receipts. Where theft or loss is concerned, you always have to make a police report (or report to the airline if that's where the problem occurs). Ensure that you keep a copy of it for your insurance company. Generally you have to bear a proportion of the cost yourself – such as the first £15–£20 of each claim. More information is given in Chapter 16, EMERGENCIES.

FREE HEALTH CARE WITHIN THE EC – FORM E111

Within the European Community a reciprocal agreement allows people from other member countries *some* free medical treatment. UK citizens obtain this via Form E111.

Getting the E111

Obtaining the E111 is now much less complicated than it used to be. Simply go to any post office (main post offices will be more likely to have them in stock than sub-post offices) and ask for the form. Fill it in and present it to the clerk together with some proof of your British citizenship, such as passport or NHS medical card – a driving licence may be acceptable. The clerk will then stamp the E111 and it will become valid immediately. You will need one for each adult in the party, but children under 16 get registered on a parent's form. Photocopies of the E111 should be accepted abroad, as well as the original.

What the E111 entitles you to

This arrangement entitles you to just the same healthcare that a Spaniard would be given – but this does not include flying you home or other special treatment. However, it *does* include pre-existing defects, pregnancy-related illness, sporting accidents, and more, which makes it a very useful supplement to travel insurance. The E111 is best thought of as a supplement in Spain.

Treatment will only be offered by doctors or hospitals that work within the state scheme. You have to have the E111 with you before they will start treatment, and should have both the original and a photocopy (to hand over) each time you go for treatment. If you call a doctor, make it clear that you have the E111 form and are expecting to be treated under the EC arrangements. If you don't make this clear from the start, you may be charged.

The E111 entitles you to some money off prescriptions, but you can expect to be charged up to 40% of their cost unless you are an EC pensioner.

The E111 is unlikely to be useful for dental treatment – you will have to pay for this.

INSURANCE FOR DRIVERS/CARS

In addition to personal and medical insurance, those driving abroad should take out adequate insurance to cover breakdown and recovery services when on the continent (see TAKING YOUR CAR, later in this chapter).

TRAVEL

Double-check bookings for accommodation, flights, ferries, trains, car-hire, etc., and make sure you have the correct times and dates. Check what is included in the price of the accommodation and confirm any requests for extra beds, etc. Any tickets or other travel documents should arrive a couple of weeks before you go.

Plan your route if you're driving and allow plenty of time to reach the port or train station if you have ferries and/or motorail booked. Ensure that you have all the necessary equipment and documentation for each country you'll be driving in (see TAKING YOUR CAR – THE PRACTIC-ALITIES, this chapter).

or. . .

Plan your trip to the airport; if you're on a very early flight and live some distance from the airport you might prefer to stay somewhere nearby the night before. For those leaving their car at the airport, make sure you park in the right car park (the long rather than the short-stay one!)

Plan your trip from the airport to your accommodation, don't leave it to chance or you may be stranded!

Find out any luggage restrictions and pack accordingly.

Make a list of emergency phone numbers you might need while away and write an itinerary, together with dates and addresses/telephone numbers, to leave with a close friend or relative.

HOLIDAY MONEY

The monetary unit is the peseta. Notes come in denominations of 100 (rare), 200 (rare), 1000, 2000, 5000 and 10,000 pesetas. Coins are in denominations of 1, 5, 10, 25, 100 and 200 pesetas. £1 = approx 200 pesetas (ptas). For banking hours, see LOCAL SERVICES in Chapter 11. There are no restrictions on the amount of money you can take into Spain, and up to 100,000 pesetas can be taken out by each person. It's a good idea, however, to change any pesetas you have left at the end of your holiday in Spain itself, where the rate of exchange is usually better than in the UK.

You will probably want to take money in several forms. Traditionally, travellers cheques have been the most popular way to carry funds on holiday, but use of credit cards and Eurocheques is now very easy, except in the most rural areas. So you can draw on your current account at home, or use a credit card, as easily in Barcelona as in Brighton (with travellers cheques, however, you are at least aware of the allocated funds being used up as each one leaves the wallet).

The main points of the most popular alternatives are covered below:

CASH

Changing some money into foreign currency before you go will mean you won't have to search for a bank as soon as you arrive or resort to the poor rates and hefty commission charges of exchanges which operate outside banking hours. For the journey itself you will need enough for drinks and snacks – if driving through France you will need French cash for tolls. Also, you should also have means to pay any French on-the-spot fines (almost F1000 for speeding!). Cash will be needed, too, to buy a few basics on arrival.

Most banks hold only limited amounts of foreign currencies, so it is safest to give them two or three days' notice of your requirements. They only supply notes, not coins. Although it would be foolish to take all your holiday money as cash, it can be annoying to be constantly changing small amounts.

TRAVELLERS CHEQUES

Travellers cheques are the most popular way of taking money abroad. They are simple, safe and, provided you take a well known brand (American Express, Thomas Cook, or from one of the big banks), are accepted almost everywhere. The cheques can be in any currency – if you take them in pesetas you only need worry about the exchange rate when you buy, rather than when you use them (although if you are going through France beware of using peseta travellers cheques, because you are then converting money yet again, and you will lose out). You can buy travellers cheques at banks, building societies and travel agents; you may be able to get them on the spot but it's advisable to order in advance, allowing about a week as they may have to be ordered from another branch. Banks charge around 1% commission on their travellers cheques but you may find that the building society rates are lower. Whoever collects the travellers cheques has to sign them in front of the cashier. On holiday, they can then only be cashed or used by that signatory – not by partners, friends or grown-up children.

To cash travellers cheques on holiday you'll need your passport as a means of identification – cashiers are always on the look out for potential thieves. Shop around for the best place to exchange them as rates and commission charges vary; as a general rule avoid late-night exchanges and hotels and stick to the larger banks where your sterling will go further.

The main advantage of travellers cheques is their refund service; facilities vary from issuer to issuer but lost or stolen cheques can usually be replaced or refunded within a reasonable period of time. Keep a separate note of the cheque numbers and the issuer's emergency telephone number. If disaster strikes this will speed up the refund process. The disadvantage is that you pay when you collect them, so the money leaves your account immediately, as cash would.

EUROCHEQUES

If you have a cheque account, you can order a book of Eurocheques and a Eurocheque guarantee card. These cheques can be used throughout Europe to buy goods or to obtain cash (although there's usually a transaction charge for the latter). Unlike UK cheques, Eurocheques have space to write in the name of the appropriate currency – so you can write a cheque in francs, pesetas, German marks or whatever, as well as in sterling. The cheque is converted into sterling at the rate of exchange prevailing on the day that the cheque is processed by your bank, and deducted from your account along with a small handling charge. Places that accept them often display a sticker (a blue and orange *ec* on a white background).

Once written and supported by a guarantee card a Eurocheque cannot be stopped – so it is extremely important to keep cheques and card apart or you could be in for heavy losses if they were stolen together.

If you know the personal identity number (PIN) for your Eurocheque card you may also be able to get money from cash dispensers, again look for the *ec*. The machines will guide you through the transaction in English, all you have to do is tap in your PIN and the amount of foreign currency you require.

Eurocheques are provided free on request by most banks although you'll be charged a small annual fee for the card. Try to order them well in advance as it may take a few weeks for the card and your PIN to reach you.

If you have an account with the Royal Bank of Scotland, a reciprocal agreement allows you to use your standard cash-point card in Banco de Santander dispensers.

CREDIT CARDS

Credit and charge cards are a useful way of paying for goods and services on holiday and, provided you can afford to pay off the balance within the specified period, they also make financial good sense. The main limitation with credit cards is that you have to stick to your pre-set spending limit although you may be able to get this raised for the duration of your holiday.

Visa, which has an arrangement with the Banco de Bilbao, is the most useful, with many more outlets than Access.

On the whole you are likely to get a better rate of exchange with a credit card or charge card than with other forms of holiday money because the credit card issuer can afford to deal at more competitive rates than the individual. Another plus is that many of the major credit card/charge card issuers operate a guarantee service for anything paid for by the card. However, don't rely solely on your credit or charge card, especially in out-of-the-way places – and not for fuel, as many petrol stations still refuse them. Credit card fraud is rife in Spain, so don't be surprised if you're asked for some form of identification (passport) when you pay. And always check that the card returned is yours – substitution of an out-of-date card is not unheard of.

TAKING YOUR CAR –
THE PRACTICALITIES

DOCUMENTS

Driving licence If you are going to drive through France, you must be 18 or over and in possession of a full EC UK driving licence. Drivers who have held their licence for less than one year must keep to a maximum speed of 90km/h (about 52mph) and display a '90' sign on the rear of the vehicle. Signs are available from most petrol stations in France.

In Spain itself, it is recommended that you carry an international driving licence. This is available from the AA and RAC to holders of a full UK driving licence who are over 18. The international licence is compulsory for holders of the green UK licence, and recommended for holders of the pink EC UK licence.

Vehicle registration document You must carry the original registration document of your vehicle. If the vehicle is not registered in your name you should carry a letter from the owner giving you permission to drive. It is routine practice in many European countries for police to check the vehicle's papers as well as the driver's licence, if they stop a car for any reason, and carrying the registration document in the car is obligatory. (If you hire a car you will be given all the documentation.)

Nationality plate You must display a GB nationality sticker on the rear of your vehicle. The oval sticker should be 17.5 cm (7 in) by 11.5 cm (4½ in) with black letters on a white background. Most insurance companies, motoring organizations and ferry companies will provide a free GB sticker.

Special note on boats It is advisable to obtain a Certificate of Registration if you are taking your boat abroad. Further details of the Certificate can be obtained from the Royal Yachting Association (see USEFUL ADDRESSES at the end of Chapter 3).

INSURANCE

Everyone driving in Spain must be insured. Your UK policy will provide overseas cover to satisfy the statutory minimum requirements in Spain. However, this is unlikely to match even third party cover in the UK – so no personal, damage, fire or theft cover is included, even if you have a fully comprehensive policy. It's best to give your insurers a ring to check their specific recommendations – it will probably be a Green Card.

Green Card These are strongly recommended for Spain (if you are planning to drive into Andorra you *must* have one), and it could prove useful in France, too. Most insurance companies will issue a Green Card free of charge for a set period. In the event of an accident, this card will assist in proving that you are insured. It will also assist in extending the cover your UK policy provides in Spain.

Bail Bond If you are involved in an accident in Spain your car may be impounded and, in serious cases, the driver detained pending investigation. Therefore it is recommended that you obtain a Bail Bond from your insurer or motoring organization before you go. The Bail Bond will often enable you to get you and your property out of custody.

Transit insurance Most car insurance provides cover for transit from UK ports. You will need to check the extent of the policy if you wish to travel on ferries outside the UK.

THE CAR

Get it serviced, and check tyres.

Headlights Your headlights should be converted for driving abroad by using either headlamp convertors or snap-on beam deflectors.

Car telephones Many countries exercise control over the importation and use of car telephones. It will probably be useless anyway. For further details contact your phone network, a motoring organization or Tourist Office.

EXTRA EQUIPMENT

It is strongly recommended that you take the following equipment when driving in Spain. The items are available from large garages, accessory shops and motoring organizations:

- red warning triangle – this is compulsory for your drive through France unless the vehicle has hazard warning lights. However, it is strongly recommended, as an accident may render the vehicle's electronics useless.
- spare bulb kit (compulsory in Spain)
- headlamp converter/deflector
- first aid kit
- left and right external mirror (the left-hand wing mirror is essential when driving on the right)
- fire extinguisher

HOLIDAY HEALTH

If you're already taking prescribed medicines make sure you have enough to last the whole holiday. Take a copy of the prescription with you just in case.

Your GP will be able to tell you whether you require any booster injections or vaccinations for the trip, will also be able to prescribe any special medical supplies you'll need and advise you on taking very young children abroad. If you or anyone in your family has a serious medical condition ask your doctor to give you a note of explanation to carry with you. A note is important in the case of allergies, too, such as to penicillin.

It's a good idea to try to carry a prescription for spectacles, too, just in case yours meet with an accident.

As far as teeth go, toothache and a hunt for a dentist can ruin a holiday, so if you're due for a check it's a good idea to have it before you go.

Most holiday ills are a result of over-exposure to the sun and unaccustomed food (see HEALTH, Chapter 11). Buy and use plenty of high-factor suncream.

FIRST AID KIT

A good first aid kit is essential on holiday. When travelling, make sure you keep it to hand. A kit should include the following – you may prefer to buy a ready-made kit and add to it yourself.

- adhesive plasters
- assorted bandages
- absorbent lint
- cotton wool
- antiseptic creams
- disinfectant
- calamine lotion/sunburn creams
- insect bite cream/repellent
- travel sickness tablets
- pain relief tablets
- scissors
- safety pins
- tweezers
- thermometer
- any medicines prescribed by your GP

HAYFEVER

Acute sufferers will probably want to head for coastal regions where on-shore winds will disperse the local pollen. Even if you think you've found a pollen-free retreat take medication with you as familiar brands may not be available.

If you'd like more information on how to plan a hayfever-free trip you can send for the *Holidays Without Hayfever Report*. Write to: Dr Jean Emberlin, Pollen Research Unit, Geography Department, Polytechnic of North London, 383 Holloway Road, London N7 8DB.

USEFUL ADDRESSES

The Department of Health's leaflet, *The Traveller's Guide To Health* (form T1), which includes further information about the E111 and claiming sickness benefits abroad, is available at post offices along with form E111. Alternatively you can write to: Health Publications Unit, No.2 Site, Heywood Stores, Manchester Road, Heywood, Lancashire OL10 2PZ or phone free on 0800 555 777. People living in Northern Ireland should should write to the address below for information, advice or form E111: Department of Health and Social Services, Overseas Branch, Lindsay House, 8–14 Callender Street, Belfast BT1 5DP.

The following may be able to offer general advice on holiday health including vaccinations; British Airways Travel Clinics: contact 071 831 5333 for details of your nearest clinic; MASTA – Medical Advisory Service for Travellers Abroad 071 631 4408; Trailfinders Medical Centre 071 938 3999; Thomas Cook Medical Centre 071 408 4157.

AT HOME

- arrange for pets to be cared for while you're away
- cancel milk/papers
- unplug all electrical appliances
- deposit special valuables in the bank
- ask someone to keep an eye on your house/water the plants, remove visible mail, etc.
- inform the DSS that you're going abroad if you're receiving any form of benefit, as it may be affected.

WHAT TO TAKE

The lists below provide an average sort of checklist – they will inevitably be too long for some readers, too short for others. It is practical to take some items below only if you are driving.

TRAVEL

- passports
- travel documents – e.g. tickets, insurance certificates
- money – travellers cheques, Eurocheques, credit cards, etc. (make a note of numbers and keep them separately). Check credit card spending limits are sufficient if you're planning to use them while away, otherwise you may prefer to leave them at home.

HEALTH AND TOILETRIES

- prescriptions – for medicines, contact lenses, glasses
- first-aid kit – see HOLIDAY HEALTH, above
- travel sickness tablets
- contraception
- tampons or sanitary towels
- contact lens solutions
- small mirror

- toiletries
- insect repellent
- sun protection
- moist wipes

USEFUL SUNDRIES

- sheets and pillowcases, unless they come with the property
- towels and beachtowels
- plastic bags
- small sewing kit
- alarm clock
- torch – at least one if you're staying in the country
- adjustable spanner (you may need it for gas bottles)
- screwdriver (there may be one in the house – but you'll know where yours is!)
- guide books/good phrase book
- back packs and/or money belts: useful for carrying maps and valuables once you're there
- holiday reading
- radio/cassette player and cassettes
- camera/films
- calculator (useful for converting currencies)
- scissors
- pen knife
- string
- continental plug adaptor for electrical appliances
- roll of lavatory paper
- pen and paper
- plug-in mosquito device (Boots and similar stores)

FOR BABIES AND YOUNG CHILDREN

- disposable nappies: but don't take supplies for the whole holiday – you'll be able to buy them when you get there
- baby toiletries
- wipes
- bibs
- feeding cup/bottles (if your baby still needs a sterilized bottle

take bottles with disposable, pre-sterilized liners/teats).
- jars of favourite baby food
- hat (with an all-round brim to shield the neck) or sun-shade
- high factor sun-protection cream: see health section
- travel games
- toys
- wellington boots (in spring and autumn)
- stick-on sun shade for the car (your own or a hire car)
- familiar bedding for very little ones

FOR THE KITCHEN

Your kitchen in Spain may be sparsely equipped, although any small essentials can always be bought. The following may prove useful, and are easier to take if you drive out. There are limits to what you can take if flying, of course.

- airtight containers
- vacuum flask
- cool bag (for picnics)
- plastic cups
- favourite sharp knife/potato peeler
- corkscrew/bottle opener
- tin-opener
- kitchen scissors
- measuring jug (calibrated in grams and ounces)
- safety matches
- foil/cling film
- a few plastic bags/dustbin bags

If you can't survive without them. . . .

- egg cups
- tea pot/strainer
- pepper mill

FOOD

It's only worth taking food to cater for personal addictions of the tea, Marmite, marmalade variety. See Chapters 6 and 7 about food in Spain.

CHAPTER FIVE

WELCOME TO SPAIN

The precise arrangements for arrival will be different from one house to another, and you should find out the procedure before you depart. Perhaps you will have to pick up keys from an office; maybe you will be met by an English agent or the caretaker; the owner might be on site; or – just as likely – you may be on your own with no one to show you around.

INVENTORY

One of the things you will have to tackle is the inventory – you may be expecting to hand over a deposit at this stage, to be returned when you leave.

The vocabulary below should help with the inventory:

abrelatas	tin opener
alfombra	carpet/rug
almohada	pillow
bandeja	tray
batidor	whisk
batidora	food mixer
bolsa de basura	bin liner
bombilla	light bulb
bombona de gas/butano	gas cylinder
brocheta	skewer
broqueta	roasting spit
cacerola	saucepan

cafetera	coffee pot
cama	bed
cama doble	double bed
cama plegable	folding bed
cazuela	casserole dish
cinecero	ashtray
coberta	saucepan lid
cocina	cooker
cogedor	dustpan
colador	colander
colador de té	tea strainer
colchón	mattress
cubiertos	cutlery
cubo	bucket
cubo de basura	dustbin
cuchara	spoon
cucharita	teaspoon
cucharón	ladle
cuchilla	large knife
cuchillo	table knife
cuchillo de carnicero	meat cleaver
cuenco	basin
desatascador	plunger
desinfectante	disinfectant
edredón	eiderdown
embudo	funnel
ensaladera	salad bowl
escoba	broom/brush
escoba mecánica	carpet sweeper
esponja	sponge
fregona	mop
funda	pillow case
garrafa	decanter
hervidor	kettle
horno	oven
huevera	eggcup
jarra	jug

lámpara (de noche)	lamp (bedside)
lejí	bleach
literas	bunk beds
manta	blanket
molinillo	coffee grinder
pala	shovel
panera	bread basket/bread bin
paño	duster
papel higiénico	lavatory paper
parilla	grill
pelador de patatas	potato peeler
percha	coat hanger
picadora	vegetable shredder
piloto	pilot light
pimentero	pepper pot
pinza para colgar ropa	clothes peg
plancha	iron
platillo	saucer
plato	plate
olla a presión	pressure cooker
rallador	grater
rodillo	rolling pin
sábana	sheet
sacacorchos	corkscrew
salero	salt cellar
salsero	gravy boat/sauce dish
sobrecama	bedspread
sopera	soup tureen
tapón	lid
taza	cup
tazón	bowl
tetera	teapot
toalla	towel
tortera	baking dish
tostadero	toaster
trapo de frega	dishcloth
trinchante	carving knife

vajilla	crockery
vinagreras	oil and vinegar cruet

If someone *is* there to show you what's what, they will most probably have a routine for showing how awkward equipment works – still, the chances are they will just have left as you discover that you only have one set of keys for six people, or some other inconvenience.

Therefore (though we're not suggesting that you ask all the questions below!) it may be worth having a quick run-through on the basics before the owner, caretaker or agent disappears, or at any rate before nightfall. (The list appears phrasebook-style in case you need to ask in Spanish.)

THINGS TO ASK THE CARETAKER/AGENT

May we check a few things before you go, please?
¿Podemos controlar alguras cosas antes que va usted, por favor?

Where's the best place to park the car?
¿Dónde está el mejor sitio para aparcar el coche?

How does this work, please?
¿Cómo se funciona este?

doors/keys	*puerta/llave*
windows	*ventana*
shutters	*contraventana*
shower	*ducha*
oven	*horno*
washing machine	*lavadora*
lights	*alumbras*
telephone	*teléfono*
water cold/hot	*agua (frío/caliente)*
air conditioning	*aire acondicionado*
lavatory	*lavabo/wáter*

Could you let us have some more . . . please?
¿Puede usted dárnos algunos más . . . por favor?

keys	*llaves*
pillows	*almohadas*
pillowcases	*fundas*
sheets	*sábanas*
blankets/duvets	*mantas/edredónes*
towels (these may not be provided, of course)	*toallas*
lavatory paper	*rollo de papel higiénico*
light bulbs	*bombillas*
coat hangers	*perchas*
cutlery	*cubiertos*
crockery	*loza*
glasses	*vasos*

Where should we put rubbish?
¿Dónde ponemos la basura?

Which way to the. . .?	*¿Dónde está la . . . ?*
Is it open tomorrow?	*¿Está abierto mañana?*
each	*cada*
supermarket/shop	*supermercade/tienda*
baker	*panadería*
bank/exchange	*banco/cambio*
post office	*oficina de correos*
petrol station	*gasolinera*
tourist office	*oficina de tourismo*
pharmacy	*farmacía*

Would you be able to arrange a babysitter for us?
¿Se puede organizar una cangura?

Could you give us the name and address of a local doctor, please?
¿Se puede dárnos el nombre y direccíon de un medico por aquí, por favor?

When does the cleaner come?
Cuándo viene la mujer de la limpieza?

Monday	*lunes*
Tuesday	*martes*
Wednesday	*miércoles*
Thursday	*jueves*
Friday	*viernes*
Saturday	*sábado*
Sunday	*domingo*
daily	*diario*
morning/afternoon	*la mañana/la tarde*

Where can we get in touch with you?
¿Cómo se pone en contacto con usted?

BASIC SHOPPING STRAIGHT AWAY

Although some houses come complete with a 'welcome pack' of basics to get you started, you will probably arrive to discover that the cupboards are bare, and might like to stock up on a few basics straight away. (You may have brought some of these with you, of course, especially if you have travelled by car.) Most of the ideas on the list below will be found in the local supermarket or a general food shop, although fruit and salad will probably be better from the market, if you find one (see Chapter 7, SHOPPING FOR FOOD).

You may decide to eat out on your first evening, so the next day's breakfast will be your main concern. If you decide to cook in, you could refer to Chapter 8, MENUS AND RECIPES, where shopping lists are included.

mineral water (sparkling/still)	*agua mineral (con gas/sin gas)*
wine	*vino*
soft drinks	*refrescos*

orange juice	*zumo de naranja*
milk	*leche*
tea	*té*
coffee	*cafe*
beer	*cerveza*
butter	*mantequilla*
margarine	*margarina*
jam	*mermelado*
bread (not Sunday)	*pane*
cheese	*queso*
eggs	*huevos*
cold meat	*fiambres*
salad	*ensalada*
vegetables	*legumbres*
fruit	*frutas*
salt	*sal*
matches	*cerillas/fósforos*
ant powder	*polvo anti-hormigas*
lavatory paper	*papel higiénico*
local map	*una mapa de la localidad*
bin liners	*bolsas de basuro*
aluminium foil	*nojuela de aluminio*
kitchen paper	*papel de cocina*
washing-up liquid	*detergente para la vajilla*
washing powder	*jabon en polvo*

See also SURVIVAL SHOPPING (Chapter 11) if you discover you have forgotten something vital.

CHAPTER SIX

EATING AND DRINKING

THE SPANISH DAY *(la dia española)*

The Spanish day starts early – and often in a bar. Families may take their *desayuno* at home, but for working people, it is common to have coffee and bread or *una tostada*, toast, on the way to work, which may start at 8 o'clock. Hot chocolate and deep-fried *churros* are another favourite. Foreigners are always surprised to find bars open for breakfast. It's a sensible use of space at a time when they are not being used for alcohol – though many Spanish are not above *una copa* for breakfast. Visitors from northern countries, where anti-drinking and driving laws are strictly enforced, are always amused to see the motorbike cops drinking their morning tots of *coñac* with black coffee: patrolling the mountains early in the day is chilly work.

Lunch is late and always a leisurely affair, for a two- or even three-hour break in the working day allows for the afternoon heat to pass. Shops and banks commonly shut at 2 p.m. (after a five-hour working morning), and the shops usually open again for a couple of hours in the evening at 5 o'clock. (The banks stay closed, usually.)

Lunch at 3 o'clock is common, and 2 o'clock is early in a restaurant. A smaller meal, *la cena*, supper, is consumed at night, usually at 9 p.m. if there are children. Restaurants in cities open at 10 and fill up at 11 o'clock at night. However in country places 9 until 10 p.m. is the common restaurant eating hour.

So long a day is sustained by two snacks. A mid-morning *aperitivo* – which might be a small beer and sandwich or a *churro* – helps to get through to lunch. Children get *una merienda* of bread with cheese or ham around 4 o'clock, and at the same time adults may have a glass of beer or a coffee and pastry, before *tapas* begin to start, at around 7 o'clock, to fill the time until dinner.

CAN WE DRINK THE WATER?
(¿Es la agua potable?)

The British abroad traditionally worry about the water, though we have recently learned that we should be at least as worried at home. In Spain, you may have trouble in the older quarters of towns, where plumbing has not been renewed, and in new housing that has been thrown up in too much of a hurry. Some Spanish water is over-chlorinated. And the water in Tarragona and Valencia *does* have a funny taste – locals in the latter say this is crucial for the perfect *paella*!

Most Spaniards are accustomed to drink bottled water with meals and these traditionally come from spas like Lanjaron, so may also do you some good. It is a pleasant and convenient habit, since the bottles can be kept chilled in the fridge.

It is not necessary to boil tap water before consuming it unless you are worried for any reason.

If you do suspect the water, remember that lettuce washed in contaminated water is one frequent cause of tummy trouble. Peel fruit (or eat oranges) rather than washing it. And remember to make ice cubes with boiled or bottled water – and refuse them when out!

Some domestic water problems come from cut-offs, which can last five hours or more. These happen without warning if there is a prolonged dry spell. If the water in the taps changes colour, this indicates it is drawing from the bottom of the tank. After the first time, it's wise to keep a large saucepan of water on the stove for emergencies (or a container if you have one) and make sure you always have a couple of bottles of mineral water in the house.

WINE, BEERS AND OTHER INTERESTING BOTTLES *(vinos y bebidas)*

WHAT IS THERE TO DRINK? *(¿Qué hay a beber?)*

Bebidas is the general word for drinks, meaning alcoholic ones in context, just as our word does. Alcoholic drinks are paced across the day. It's common to drink vermouth *(vermú)* before lunch since this is the main meal of the day, and is likely to be followed by time for repose or sleep. In the evenings, the men tend to go to the *tapas* bars to relax after work and to drink wine or sherry.

One thing evident is a national passion for coffee. This is always made the same way – dark and strong; the difference is in the way it is served. At breakfast *café con leche* in a large cup is mellowed by more than its own volume of hot milk. After dinner a demi-tasse is *café solo*, but you can also choose to have the same quantity of coffee served in a glass 'short': *un café corto*, or *un cortado*, where there will be room for a small amount of milk. *Descafeinado* is available, but is always instant coffee. In summer you can also order *un blanco y negro*, a glass of milky iced coffee, heavily scented with cinnamon, which is drunk through a straw.

Herb teas are more popular than the tea leaf. Camomile tea, *(una manzanilla)* is traditional and you will see sacks of the flowers in grocer's stores. But don't confuse it with the palest, most delicate of sherries, which has the same name. Tea *(té)* is drunk without milk; but you can ask for it either *con limón* (with lemon) or *con leche* (with milk). Herb teas are known as *infusiones* and popular flavours are mint *(poleomenta)*, lime *(tila)* and lemon verbena *(hierba luisa)*. You can also order iced tea *(té helado)*.

NON-ALCOHOLIC DRINKS *(refrescos)*

The word *refrescos* has delightfully cool overtones and means cool drinks, and implies a soft one. If you are buying *refrescos* to drink immediately, ask for *bebidas frías*, ready-chilled ones.

Bottled water is the cheapest bought drink. The big question with water, however, is *con gas o sin gas*, with or without bubbles. The big sellers are Solares, Font Vella and Lanjaron. Vichy Catalan is the leading bubbly water.

Spanish lemonades *(gaseosos)* are fizzy. The ubiquitous La Casera is colourless and sweet, nearest to the old-fashioned 'cream' sodas. Fruit juice is *zumo de fruta* and popular flavours are *naranja*, *limón* and *pomelo*, orange, lemon and grapefruit. To get freshly-squeezed juice add *natural*. You can also make your own good old-fashioned freshly-squeezed citrus fruit. Every Spanish kitchen should have a lemon squeezer. One orange and half a lemon (or whole lemon) with ice, sugar to taste and water makes the pleasantest of drinks, and also a cheap one.

Fruit syrups for diluting with water or soda – and often something stiffer – are available in all the bars. Rives make a colourful series, including the green Kiwi, passion fruit SLP and *granadína*, from pomegranates.

BEER AND CIDER *(cerveza y sidra)*

The 'real ale' people don't like Spanish beer, complaining that it is too light and gassy, but it is well suited to Spanish weather. *Cerveza*, the Spanish lager, is a better quality than the international lagers that many people drink at home. But you can buy imported beers *(cerveza extranerja)* everywhere at a higher price.

Beer is often a better choice than wine in the summer heat. The best local one is San Miguel *especial*; look also for Aquila and Victoria. Mahou is the best bitter, and less gassy. Draught beer has been on sale in Madrid since the beginning of the century, when 'beer gardens' were introduced.

In the green northern part of Spain apple trees hug the mountains. In Asturias cider replaces wine, while the Basques claim to have invented it. In the local cider shops (*sidrerias*), you can drink, and eat in the intervals.

INTERNATIONAL APERITIFS *(aperitivos)*

Though we tend to drink drier aperitifs and save sweeter, stronger wines for after dinner, the Spanish are like the French in enjoying sweet aperitifs. The Spanish firm of Larios is the world's second largest producer of gin, while sizeable quantities of vermouth are made in Barcelona. In Mallorca, which has an English tradition, gin is drunk 'on the rocks' (*ginebra con hielo*), and also with a lemon slice, ice and soda (*en pallofa*) – and drunk strong! It is also drunk with sweet mixers.

All the standard international drinks are made in Spain and many variants, like Spanish vodka, are perfectly acceptable to the British palate once mixed, and are considerably cheaper. Although imported whiskies are available, you may still want to try DYC, the local brew. A whisky and soda is *un whiskysifon*. The leading brand of whisky on the continent is Ballantines, which will jolt a Johnnie Walker, Famous Grouse or Teachers drinker!

SHERRY *(jerez)*

Sherry is a mispronunciation of the place name Jerez de la Frontera, just north of Cadiz, in the south-west. It makes exceptional fortified wines and is one of the few places in Spain with a long tradition of fine wines.

We think of dry sherries as aperitifs, but in Spain *fino* counts as a white wine, and is drunk through an evening's *flamenco*, or accompanies fish. It's one of the world's great white wines, and remarkably cheap for the quality.

Manzanillas (which means camomile) are the driest and most delicate sherries. Right at the top end of the market – but still around a tenner – try sherries from *un almacenista*, an individual maturer and bottler. *Amontillado* is a *fino* that has been matured to become softer and darker. It is usually less dry. *Palo cortado* is rarer because it occurs by accident. It is

79

darker than *amontillado* and sweeter. *Olorosos* are generally sweeter, sometimes reminiscent of port and excellent after dessert.

Rather similar tasting wines are made in nearby Montilla. Look for *fino* from Montilla, a little cheaper than sherry. Alvear has an excellent brand called CB which is much used in the south for cooking and drinking.

RED WINE *(vino tinto)*

Vino corriente is what the Spanish drink – and what you will find in your supermarket. Most Spanish wine is bottled young, rather than being left to mature in barrels – almost half of the production in famous districts like Rioja. These reds have a softer, drier and fruitier taste than French wines, without the tannin that makes ageing possible. Their freshness makes them remarkably pleasant drinking.

The biggest seller is Campos Viejo's San Ascensio *2° año sin crianza*, which means second year, without barrel ageing. Close behind it come the third-year wines, *3° año*, from the state firm CUNE, and Banda Azul from Federico Paternina, with a blue band across the label.

However, it is the barrel-aged wines that are so distinctive in Spain. Maturing in wood casks is practised the world over, but it is the hint of vanilla from American oak that is the fingerprint of Spanish wine, and of Rioja in particular. *Crianza* means aged in wood: a minimum of a year for red wine and six months for white and rosé. *Reserva* (4 years old) is the quality that is often exported, and modest ones end up back home in supermarkets at around £4 a bottle.

The best Riojas are Gran reservas (six years and up) and their quality usually exceeds wine in the same price bracket made in France or Italy. Rioja is Spain's premier wine district, and house style and brand names are very important, for the *bodegas* (wine forms) are allowed to buy in other grapes and to blend their wines. For this reason there are few *château*-bottled wines. Affordable exceptions are Marqués de Murietta at Castillo Ygay and Torres' Castell de Fransola.

Some Spanish *bodegas* favour the old-style wines, and like them heavy with vanilla. The three big names here are Marqués Riscal, Marqués de Murrieta and Muga. Wines from the cooler, higher Rioja Alta are more likely to be aged. Try one of the big ones like Viña Ardanza, which can have an amazing vanilla aroma, or the dark-tasting Viña Tondonia from López de Heredia. Wines from the Rioja Alavesa are sometimes more full-bodied, and Viña Pomal, for instance, has cigarbox flavours.

French grapes were first introduced in Ribera del Duero and any Cabernet Sauvignon wine will be a good, but more expensive, choice. You could try one from Raimat in Lérida (or their Abadia). Torres Gran Coronas is another popular choice. In Ribera itself the affordable choice is the local, light Peñafiel.

Navarra, next door to Rioja, makes pleasant fruity reds. The younger wines have been likened to Beaujolais. Sonomora is the up and coming area in Aragon, making slightly lighter reds in a region better known for the hefty purplish Cariñena.

Classic full-bodied reds, like Scala Dei, are made in Priorato, inland from Tarragona on the east coast. Valdepeñas, at the southern plain of La Mancha (Spain's wine lake) is easily distinguished by the old Ali Baba wine jars standing by the road; these are still used for wine-making. Here some good wines are made with Cenibel, the local name for the classic Rioja grape.

In the north west El Bierzo and Leon make pleasant reds, while the big Toro is the oldest red wine in Spain. Reputedly Columbus took casks on the Santa Maria. Here in the north of country you will also find *clarete*. Nothing to do with clarets, this is simply a lighter style of wine than the red *tinto*, made by mixing black and white grapes.

In the south of the country and the east coast, the sun is an enemy of decent red wines. But if you are on holiday here, try SAVIN's red wine, which has the expertise of Spain's biggest wine firm behind it. Or reds from Utiel-Requena, inland from Valencia.

ROSÉ WINE *(rosada)*

Some excellent rosé wines are made in Spain. In Navarra they make up 40% of production: the name to look for here is Gran Feudo.

On the south and east coast there are several good *rosadas*. These are much lighter and fresher, and I think a much better buy, than the reds of the region. An unusual one called Rosat Scala Dei is made in Priorato, while the delicate light wines from Utiel-Requena (Valencia) are among best in Spain. Look also for cherry-coloured *rosadas* from the tiny Ampurdan, the wine region of the Costa Brava.

WHITE WINE *(vino blanco)*

A dry, 'sherry' taste is typical of many of Spain's traditional whites: 'sharp and strong as goat's cheese', Laurie Lee called them. The sun turns the sugar into alcohol, making wine that is very dry and deep in colour. The Cadiz Chiclana, Extremaduran Cañamero and Montilla *finos* are better examples of this, while the rough whites of La Mancha fuel the *tascas*, or bars, of working-class Madrid.

These wines were never popular with foreigners. In order to create an export market, therefore, Spain started making fresh clean whites, that were rather like French white wines. A leading producer was the Torres firm in Penedès, in Catalonia. This is Spain's second most important wine region. Try any of the Viña Sol whites – the cheapest one is lemony, the Green Label sophisticated. Viña Esmeralda makes a pleasant, sweet aperitif.

Some fresh whites are made with traditional grapes. 'Green' wine is made from the *alberiño* grape in the far Galician west. Probably the best accompaniment to shellfish of all Spanish wines, it is dry with a bit of sparkle and seems almost German in character. In Ruedo fruity whites are made from the local Verdejo, and these wines are not very strong in alcohol. Look for Marqués de Riscal. Marqués de Allela, north of Barcelona, supplies that city with a delicate white wine with a prickly edge.

Most Riojan wines are no longer barrel-aged, and these are light and fresh. The first, and still the best, of these is the Marqués de Caceres; try also Montecillo's Vino Cumbrero.

However, oak-ageing continues in Rioja and elsewhere in a few *bodegas*, for it adds an extra dimension to big, buttery wines. To sample these, try Marqués de Murrieta Ygay *crianza* and *reserva blanco* and Bodegas Riojana's white Monte Real. And the state firm of CUNE has managed to have it both ways, by producing a wine that has a modest amount of oak, yet has some fruity freshness! The result is the popular Monopole.

SPARKLING WINES *(cavas)*

Spain, rather than France, is the world's largest producer of sparkling wines made by the champagne method, acquiring their sparkle in the bottle. *Champaña* is the real French champagne, while *champán* means champagne-style, and these are excellent value for money. Freixenet, for example, in a black bottle, is becoming a well-known brand in Britain. The Spanish like their sparkling wines sweet, so if this is not a taste you share, look for *brut* on the bottle. Raimat now make a sparkler exclusively from Chardonnay grapes, while Codorníu (the largest Spanish firm) make an excellent Chardonnay. Most *cavas* are made at San Sadurní de Noya in Catalonia. *Espumosa* means any sparkling wine, so automatically a lesser one. *Granvas* are the inferior ones, made in steel tanks under pressure.

DESSERT WINE

Spain really only makes one good white wine of the Sauternes sort, Masia Bach's Extrísimo *blanco semidulce*, pale with a drop of honey in the finish. It goes well with *crema catalana*.

In the heat of the south and eastern coasts muscat grapes flourish, producing wines that smell of the grapes. Moscatel de Valencia is at the lighter end. Moscatels from Malaga are darker and like sipping sultanas; they were known in the 19th century as the perfect 'ladies' wine (sweet and very strong).

There are several grades of these, some in wicker-covered flasks. Malaga *dulce* (sweet) is the nicest, for the grapes shrivel and concentrate before they are pressed. The result tastes somewhere between toffee and sultanas and is an excellent way to end a meal, instead of pudding. Málaga Lágrima ('from tears'), so called because the grapes drip rather than being pressed, is more like a liqueur. Pedro Ximénez is luscious grape, also made into a sweet wine of a dark treacly colour. Juice from this grape is added to *oloroso* to turn it into a 'cream' sherry; try Pedro Domecq's Viña 25. Malvasía is another good dessert wine.

FORTIFIED WINES *(generosos y rancios)*

Un generoso is a fortified wine, dry or sweet, drunk before or after a meal, made like an *oloroso* sherry, and so aged in casks with access to the air. They are made in Huelva, called Condado Viejo, and round the country in places like Rueda in the north-west and Ampurdan in the east. *Un rancio* is a mellowed, fortified dessert wine, also drunk as an aperitif – *vi ranci* in Catalan.

Tarragona produces the 20-year-old Fondillon, a copper-coloured dessert wine, full of nutty toffee flavour. Tarragona is also famous for its fortified dessert wines, which are also referred to as *Tarragona classicos*.

BRANDY AND DISTILLED LIQUORS *(coñac y destilados)*

Brandy far outsells sherry in Spain, playing the dessert rôle and is a common way to end a meal. Most brandies are made in Jerez – they were originally used for fortifying sherry. However, Catalonia also produces French-style brandies, notably Mascaró and Torres' Black Label. At the cheap end, Pedro Domecq's Fundador is popular with foreigners because it is grapey, though roughish but not too sweet.

However, the Spanish like after-dinner brandies that are caramelized and have added syrup, and so are markedly sweet and perfumed. Osborne makes two of the most popular brands. Magno is the big seller in the middle price-range, smoother and aromatic. Veterano is a close second, popular also for the advertisements that promote it, magnificent outlines of a black bull which so enhance the southern skyline.

Ponche in a silver bottle, sometimes with no label, will be a herbalized and sweetened old brandy, often with an orange taste. De Soto and Caballero are well-known brands.

Aguardiente strictly means any distilled liquor. The popular *aguardiente de orujo* is a rough grape brandy, made by distilling the already-fermented pips and skins left from wine-making. This makes it the equivalent of the French *marc*. In bars it is commonly asked for as *orujo*, and may be the local brew, round 80% proof, poured from unmarked bottles.

Anis is a leading flavour as it is in France. Chinchón, near Madrid, is a well-known brand name of this colourless liquor, and also makes a *dulce*, sweeter version. Anís de Mono is another.

LIQUEURS *(licores)*

Pacharán is Spain's top generic liqueur, drunk before or after dinner – and almost unknown outside the country. It looks like brandy – and is served in a brandy glass on the rocks. It is made from sloes in the same tradition as sloe gin, and is flavoured with *anis*. Pacharán is perfumed and sweet – and the kind of drink that doesn't translate at all well back to Britain's foggy shores. The taste is on a parallel to the local *sol y sombra* (literally sun and shade), made from a double slug of *anis* to one of brandy – but far less lethal. The red-tinted Zoco is the best-known brand, although the best I have had was Patxaran Alor from Navarra, in an Armagnac-shaped bottle.

If you like your sweet liqueur not too sweet, Triple sec in the square bottle is one to try. Bebidas is the name of one popular line of fruit liqueurs – peach *bebidas de melocotón* is not for the children. Chartreuse is made in Tarragona, which became the home of the herb liqueurs when the monks were expelled from France. Local tastes are for Calisay, which is quinine-based, and Liquor 43 *(cuaranta y tres)*. This liqueur is clear, golden and sweet, flavoured with vanilla, but with a lingering taste.

PUNCHES AND ALCOHOLIC COFFEES *(ponches y cafés)*

Sangria must be one of the world's best-known punches *(ponches)*, made of red wine, citrus juices and ice, then diluted with soda water or lemonade. Classic recipes add brandy to make up the strength again – not recommended when it's hot. In a restaurant these are often disappointing affairs, sticky and sweet, but they are easy and refreshing to make at home. Pleasant regional variations include the white-wine *zurro* in La Mancha and the Basque *linoyada*, half red and white wine, poured onto home-made lemon syrup.

There are also some punches that will blow your legs away like *queimada*, made from flamed *aguardiente*, with coffee beans added. In Mallorca, with its strong English tradition, *punys d'ous*, a winter egg punch that has definite overtones of the English navy, is made from rum, lemons, eggs and sugar. *Zurracapote*, a hot red wine punch like our bishop, is made with Rioja, cinnamon and brandy.

At the end of a meal a little tot of *anis* or brandy goes into a *café solo* – to make *un carajillo*. Or try the Catalan *cremat*: a potent mixture in which brandy and rum – sometimes four liquors – are flamed, then coffee added.

EATING OUT

WHERE SHALL WE EAT? *(¿Dónde comemos?)*

Spain is an ideal country for eating out. One reason is that the same type of menu is served in the cheapest and the most expensive restaurants (except for the smart *nouvelle cuisine* establishments). So the gourmet can look for interesting dishes and you can always find something for children.

In restaurants at most holiday resorts dress is quite casual, even in quite expensive ones. However nudity, sandy feet and the style of dressing that involves more splits than cloth may

cause comment, and even rejection. Beach nudity may be a challenge, but very short shorts or sunbathing tops (on women) and shirtlessness on men can be inappropriate elsewhere.

The least formal watering holes are small bars with standing room only. In town *tabernas* sell cheap wine and other drinks. *Tascas* are similar: you will find these on the beach, a bar with food on it for those standing drinking.

Bars, where you will find *tapas*, are convivial establishments for meeting friends and are able to supply food and drink from breakfast to supper if you wish. In sherry country in the south look out for open *bodegas*. Strictly these are take-away liquor shops, but because they offer samples from an assortment of barrels, they are also wonderful places to drink a selection and eat shellfish.

Cafes and *cafeterias* tend to be just that, offering coffee (and beer) as their main fare. Like coffee bars, they are a modern concept and sell only minor snacks. For a midday meal or a stifling evening *un merendero* is a good bet. They tend to be pleasantly casual, serving food outside on a terrace, and frequently specialize in sea food on the coast.

Inland, and in more remote places that have no restaurants, there may be inns of various sorts: a *fonda* or the humbler *posada*, serving simple food.

Restaurantes come in all grades. You should try to visit one *parador* if you are anywhere near one. This is a hotel in the state-run hotel chain. They are often housed in historic buildings – there are numerous castles and even ex-monasteries on the list. As a day off self-catering they are perfect – and this is the best way to try them out. They also attract some of the best chefs and are very cool and lavishly spacious. They are expensive – but only by Spanish standards – so it is possible to run up a bill of £15 or even £20 for adults, if you splash out – but they serve good regional food.

The Spanish star-rating system for restaurant food is run by Gourmetour, marking restaurants from 1 to 10. The cities of Madrid, Barcelona and San Sebastian are all famed for their restaurants. These may be influenced by international cuisine and standards, but they nevertheless remain very Spanish; even *nouvelle cuisine (nueva cocina)* is very Spanish.

If your taste is more for local food – as mine is – many restaurants these days advertise *platos tipicos* – typical local dishes. You can ask if there are any local specialities (*¿Hay especialidades locales?*) If dishes are labelled *de la casa*, they should be home-made.

Spanish meals are usually a slow affair, comprising several courses, with waits. Any dish that is advertised *en cargo*, cooked to order, as *paella* should be, is likely to take longer still. If you are in a hurry, say so at the beginning: *tenemos prisa.* You would do best to choose the main dish of the day, *el plato del día*, because it will be waiting ready. Have it, perhaps, with a salad.

Many cake shops, *pastelerías*, also have a couple of tables, where you may sit and eat their wares on the premises, with a herb tea, or a lemonade. Sometimes these even advertise themselves as *un salon de té*.

TAPAS

Two rules apply in Spain: don't drink without eating – and don't eat without drinking. The food in a tapas bar is there 'to keep you on your feet'; *tente en pie*, the locals say. Spanish food genius really flourishes in the *tapas* bar. It seems the answer to all social problems of eating, and offers a variety of food so freshly cooked and appetizing that these bars shame most English pubs.

Many Spaniards start their social day here, with a coffee for breakfast, or a snack, after an early start. *Tapas* make a good light lunch for anyone planning to eat a main meal later. The variety of *tapas* available is laid out on top of the bar for inspection. Portions are scooped onto little dishes, or whisked into a microwave, for reheating. In big cities like Santander, Cadiz and Madrid, locals go on *tapas* crawls, from bar to bar. *Ir de pinchos* it is called, for *pinchos*, a morsel on a cocktail stick, has become synonymous with *tapas*.

In the old days simple *tapas* – olives, a few cooked chickpeas or squares of bread and *chorizo* – were free, offered with the drinks. And such small morsels may still come unasked. However you will normally have to pay for a *tapa*. *Una ración* brings a fair-sized plate of food.

The simplest things are some of the most delicious, black-rinded Manchego cheese with bread, and *aceitunas aliñados*. These marinated olives are far superior to the brine-cured ones sold back home.

But the high point is raw ham (*jamón serrano*) hanging in a phalanx over the bar: often deep red, carved thinly along the bone, chewy, succulent and irresistible. The best are *pata negra*, from wild pigs with black trotters, and the names of Jabugo, Trevélez and Montánchez are honoured throughout the country.

Simple cooked dishes include fried cheese slices (*queso frito*) (see MENUS AND RECIPES, Chapter 8) and squid rings of deep-fried *calamares*, which are so identified with the Mediterranean coast. Other popular choices are battered fried prawns, known colloquially as 'prawns in mackintoshes' (*gambas en gabardina*), choux puffs with cheese (*buñelos de queso*) or olives, croquettes based on bechamel (*croquetas*) with many additions, and *flaminquines*, deep fried rolls based on ham and cheese.

More exotic things are strictly regional. In the Basque country and along the Cantabrian coast there is *txangurro*, crab potted or grilled in scallop shells, and little batter fritters called *kokotxas*, which are the cheeks of hake. A winter speciality is baby eels (*anguilas*) tossed in garlic and chilli and eaten with a wooden fork. The Cadiz area specializes in fried fish (*pescaito frito*) and a particular favourite on the whole south coast are batter-fried baby fish (*chanquetes*).

But one of the charms of the *tapas* bar for many is that it offers plain things with succulent sauces. This is why such bars make convenient places for feeding children. Kidneys in sherry (see MENUS AND RECIPES) is a universal favourite, and across the country you will find tripe (*callos*) with or without chickpeas: try it and be surprised.

THE MENU *(la lista)*

The multi-coursed menu of soup and *entremés* followed by egg or rice, then fish or meat, winding up with fruit coffee and liqueurs, is common throughout the country, even though dishes are regional. The number of plates doesn't mean that the portions are small. Far from it. Plates of vegetables could well be classified as stews back home.

By law every restaurant is obliged to offer a set menu of at least two courses with wine *(los platos combinados)* and these are very good value for money. They are also a good guide to local fare, as this is what the regulars will choose. Ask if there is a children's menu *(un menu para niños)*.

STARTERS *(entreméses)*

A little *aperitivo* may be served with drinks before you reach the table. But the same dish, served in a larger portion becomes *un entremés*.

Salads *(ensaladas)* are very common: like lettuce, tomato, olive and onion, or the favourite of *pimiento* and anchovies (see MENUS AND RECIPES) or green beans. *Un ensalada mixta* will almost certainly contain canned tuna and hard-boiled egg. The rest will depend on the ambition of the chef.

A much older salad is *pipirrana* which contains all the summer vegetables chopped and chilled (see MENUS AND RECIPES). The surprises are the salt-cod salads, sophisticated textures and tastes like *esqueixada*, a mixture of red pepper and tomato shreds with *bacalao* and *remojón*, a salad of oranges and salt cod with olives.

In Catalonia they do delicious arranged salads with a mixture of everything and anything, including canned sardines and sausage, (the local name for salad is *amanida*). *Un entremés de carne* is a good way to sample all the local sausages, especially in places like Vich or Extremadura which are famed for them.

SOUPS *(sopas)*

Cold soups *(sopas frías)* are a brilliant Andalucian invention. *Gazpacho rojo*, iced tomato, cucumber and peppers soup, made creamy with bread and oil, and delicately flavoured with garlic and vinegar, is now made all over Spain. In Madrid it may contain mayonnaise, while the Malaga version, *ajo blanco*, is made from white almonds.

Hot garlic soups *(sopas de ajo)* are something to try when you have been caught in a thunderstorm, or are simply short of cash. They are powerful – traditionally served to the bridal pair on their wedding night to keep up their strength! – but made of little more than bread, garlic, paprika and hot water, perhaps with a beaten egg.

The star soup is *caldo*. Properly made it is the broth from the pot in which meat has simmered all day. This is the origin of consommé with sherry, with names like *sopa viña AB* here. (Initials are a good sign with anything to do with sherry.) *Sopa de picadillo* is another pleasant, clear soup, with chopped ham and mint in it (good for hangovers), while *sopa de fideos* is what we call chicken noodle.

Sopa de mariscos, shellfish soup, is one of the big bargains, especially on the northern and eastern coasts. Every restaurant serves it and fish soups *(sopas de pescados)* too, in hundreds of local versions. *Gazpachuelo* is a version with vinegar, or sometimes creamy potato and mayonnaise. Clam and mussel soups such as *de almejas o de mejillones* are also common (see MENUS AND RECIPES, Chapter 8).

Anything described as a *potaje* is a much heavier affair, chock full of vegetables, and almost a stew.

EGGS *(huevos)*

Eggs form a separate course, even in expensive restaurants. *Tortilla* is the local omelette, not a creamy folded affair, but a thick cake with erect sides. Potato and onion are the favoured fillings, but ham and prawns are common.

Scrambled egg is a different affair in Spain, stirred in a pan with oil. Don't miss *revuelto de trigueros*, egg and wild asparagus, in spring and in autumn *revueltos de setas*, with wild mushrooms. The Basque version is a moist red omelette in the French style, with softened red peppers, called *piperada*.

Fried eggs, *huevos fritos*, are served with fried potatoes and *chorizo* in for example *huevos a la cordobesa*, or with garlic croûtons (*migas*), making almost a breakfast dish.

RICE AND PASTA *(arroces y pastas)*

Introduced by the Arabs, medium-grain rice is most famous in the flavourful mixtures of the Valencian *paella. El caldero* on the east coast is a fishy soup of rice. Another Valencian dish is *arroz abanda*, literally 'rice apart', where the rice is served alone first, then the fish whose stock gave it so much flavour follows, hot or cold, with *alioli* (see MENUS AND RECIPES). *Arros amb crosta* is an oven dish, with an egg crust hiding a scented mixture of rice with poultry, sausage and meat balls.

There are several interesting pasta dishes too. Italians staffed Spanish restaurants in the 19th century, and introduced lasagne and canelloni.

VEGETABLES *(legumbres)*

Although there are many Spanish vegetable dishes, not all of them are suitable for vegetarians, for they are flavoured with cured pork and sausages and cooked with pork fat, to make them richer.

Every part of the country boasts of the local dried beans, usually under local names. Sausage (*chorizo*) is a favoured partner, for the paprika in it is a wonderful vegetable flavouring. Sausage goes with chickpeas (*garbanzos*) and fresh beans too, like *habas con butifarra* in Catalonia. Beans or peas (*guisantes*) with fried ham are also found everywhere.

Less filling are red pepper salads or mushrooms cooked with garlic (*champiñones al ajillo*). Try spinach with grapes and pinenuts (*espinacas con uvas y piñones*). Aubergines, with Moorish flavourings of cinnamon or cumin, are often stuffed (see MENUS AND RECIPES). *Samfaina* is the local ratatouille, while a mixture of tomato, courgette and onion is called *pisto* here, often combined with eggs and made with pumpkin in the south. Tomatoes are stuffed (*tomates rellenos*) with nuts and spinach or minced meats. And not to be missed are wonderful smoky vegetables from the grill, like the Catalan *escalivada* and the onion *calçotada*.

FISH AND SHELLFISH (*pescados y mariscos*)

Fish and shellfish are plentiful, even inland, and the choice is huge. They may be *gambas al ajillo* (simply fried with garlic), or *almejas o mejillones a la marinera* (clams or mussels opened simply in wine). Octopus is done the festive way, *pulpo a feria* – as a salad with paprika oil. Line-caught squid are made into *chipirones en su tinta*, served in their own ink in Basque country.

Perhaps the most luxurious dish is *langosta con alioli*, grilled spiny lobster with the wonderful Catalan garlic sauce, which is like a garlic mayonnaise. Another inspired Catalan mixture is *langosta con pollo*, lobster with chicken, and lobster with (not sweet!) chocolate sauce (*langosta con chocolate*).

On the east coast there are several stunning mixed-fish dishes, such as the operatically named *zarzuela*, and *susquet*, both of which star shellfish. However the single most-eaten dish in the country is Basque *merluza a la vasca*: hake is cooked in a sauce that also contains mussels or prawns and often a quantity of parsley or peas too, that give it its other name, *salsa verde*, green sauce.

On the Atlantic coast layered *calderetas* (fish stews) are favoured, perhaps with *cachelada*, the local new potatoes, and possibly with cider too. The Basque favourite tuna, *bonito*, is stewed in *marmitako* with two sorts of peppers, while swordfish is grilled or kebabed plainly as *brocheta de pez espada*. The fine Galician white wine is used as a sauce for sole or turbot (*lenguado o rodaballo al albariño*).

Freshwater trout are often stuffed with or wrapped in ham, like *truchas a la navarra*, while *salmón a la ribereña* are salmon steaks with ham. Trout is also excellent pickled (*trucha escebechada*) (see MENUS AND RECIPES).

Simple frying sets off most fish, like flat *gallo*, served with lemon or skate with paprika (*raya en pimientón*). Look particularly for *fritura de pescado*, a fry-up of mixed fish, and fans of fresh anchovies (*boquerones*), in Malaga. Deep-frying is a high art in Spain – try *merluza a la romana*.

Salt cod is a national passion, most famous in the Basque *bacalao a la vizcaina*, cooked with piquant peppers and chillies or in *pil pil*, a rather gelatinous white sauce of oil and fish juices.

BIRDS AND GAME *(aves y caza)*

Chicken (*pollo*) is ubiquitous and excellent, most famous when fried with ham, tomato and red and green peppers *en chilindrón*. Duck is at its very best with bitter orange juice to cut the fat, *pato a la sevillana*. Olives have the same effect in duck *con aceitunas*. Catalans also favour fruit, duck with figs (*anec amb figues*).

Small wild birds are traditionally the cheaper choice. *Codornices al ajillo* are quails pot roasted with garlic or served up in green peppers *en zurrón*, which means 'in the hunter's knapsack'. *Perdices a la navarra* is one of the many partridge dishes with gravy containing chocolate as its magic ingredient. Pigeon with grapes and pinenuts (*pichon con pasas y pinones*) is another successful combination.

Wild rabbit is very popular; in *conejo en adobo* it is stewed with thyme. Snails containing rosemary also accompany rabbit in *conejo con carecoles*.

MEAT *(carnes)*

Roasts from the big bread ovens, beehive Moorish-looking affairs, are the highpoint of Spanish meat cookery. *Lechazo* is a milk-fed lamb, called *ternasco* in Navarra, and sucking pig (*cochinillo*), famous round Segovia, are often so small that one or two people are served a whole leg.

In any bourgeois restaurant you will be amazed by the size of the steaks (*solomillos*) and *chuletónes*, vast beef chops on the bone. Eaten without vegetables too, for the middle classes eat a heavy meat diet. Best of all are tiny lamb chops, grilled over vine prunings (*chuletas de cordero al sarmiento*).

Pork plays a central role in the kitchen. The *matanza*, the pig slaughtering in November, provides sausages to eat through the year. Every region makes its own, with associated traditional dishes. Pork chops, and loin (*lomo*) remain Spain's most familiar meats.

The national dish is *cocido*, a pot of many meats, slow simmered to produce both meats and a wonderful broth. There are also a number of stews, but sadly the process of making them is time-consuming and now they are not often found.

DESSERTS (*postres*)

Fruit ends most Spanish meals, but the traditional desserts should be tried. Caramel custard (*flan*) is the national pudding. A better version is *tocino de cielo*. Toffee-topped and looking like a slab of bacon (hence the name), it is made from egg yolks and syrup, a melt-in-the-mouth morsel. Chilled custards (*natillas*) are popular, sometimes topped with meringue, but the best is *crema catalana*, perhaps the original *crème brulée*. *Menjar blanca* is a much older, Arab almond cream.

Milk and cream are largely reserved for puddings, like the Asturian rice pudding (*arroz con leche*), heavily scented with cinnamon and lemon. *Leche frita*, literally fried milk, is squares of cold custard, coated and fried and served hot or cold. Asturias is also famed for liquorous *crêpes* (*filloas*). Cheesecakes are made in the Basque country, called *quesada*, as well as in the Balearic Isles: look for *flaón* and *greixonera de brossat*.

Some Spanish ices are not good, though *sorbete de limón*, lemon sorbet, is always refreshing. Commercial ices are less fun than the *tarrinas* (earthenware pots) they are served in. Muscatel is good (see MENUS AND RECIPES, Chapter 8), while the best ice cream cake (*tarta helada*), is the triple-layered *tarta al whisky*, with a brittle caramel top.

Pears baked in red wine were invented in Galicia, and peaches in red wine (*melocotón en vino tinto*) are even more delicious. Fried bananas (*platanos fritos*) are a Canary Isles speciality. Stewed prunes on holiday? But liqueur-soaked *anis ciruelas pasas* might change your mind. *Zurracapote* is a good Basque dried fruit compote.

Spanish cakes can be rather heavy. Best-known is the brown gipsy's arm (*brazo gitano*), sponge rolled up with custard (*cremadina*) in the middle. *Bizcocho* is sponge cake, best when *borrachos* ('drunken') in squares soaked with syrup or wine. Almond tart (*tarta santiago*) can be very good if moist and lightly cooked.

THE BILL (*la cuenta*)

Ask for the bill (*la cuenta, por favor*). *Servicio incluido* means that service is included. This is a potentially tricky word, since *servicio*, singular, is service, but the plural, *los servicios*, are toilets.

Tips are expected – 10% is a good guide, but the amount declines as the bill mounts. Once you have reached 10,000 pesetas, you can think in terms of the minimum of 5%. If you are sitting down in a *tapas* bar, it is customary to leave a coin (or put it in the staff box on the bar if there is one). Cloakroom attendants expect 25–100 pesetas.

Restaurants (and hotels) are obliged to keep a complaints book. Persistent lack of co-operation can often be cured just by asking for the *hoja de reclamación*.

CHAPTER SEVEN

SHOPPING FOR FOOD

Look at your storage space before you go shopping. There is unlikely to be a large fridge, and you may find that the bathroom is the only cold place. So don't stock up with a mass of stuff that you don't intend to eat for a few days and that needs refrigerating. Make sure you eat food in ripeness order – or you will pick the best and chuck the rest. Trays of peaches quickly attract a hovering cloud of small flies.

THE MARKET *(el mercado)*

¿Qué dias hay mercado? What day is the market? Ask your neighbours when you arrive. The market is where you will find food in season and at its cheapest. Besides the colour, life and fun of it all, it is the best possible way to see what is on offer, and at what sort of prices. It's the place for bulk buy bargains, so stock up with items that keep, like olives and onions.

A fair amount of ready-prepared food can be had in the market, although apart from frozen food, Spaniards are not into take-away dinners. From the sizzling vats of oil over their gas burners come *churros*, rings and squiggles of batter, piped directly into the oil and sold sprinkled with sugar in papers or linked together by a grass tied through the hoops. In the south and east there are other fried doughnuts or puffs, like *bunyols*, and there are little spicy meat or fish-filled pasties (*empanadillas*) in the province of Murcia.

The roast chicken stall (*pollos asados*) is also a part of the holiday weekend scene. Roasted on spits in racks, and well-basted with pork fat, chickens are a good buy. Locals often take their own pot to collect them, for the foil box (*la bandera*) in which they are otherwise packed is extra.

THE SHOP *(la tienda)*

The corner shop (*una tienda de comestibles*) is alive and well in Spain, and there is likely to be one near any holiday letting complex. Licensing laws are simpler than at home and many of these little (and not so little) shops handle groceries, milk, bread, fresh vegetables and alcohol, and may have fresh meat and yoghurt too, if there is a cool cabinet. *Una mantequería* is a general grocery, and *una verdulería* is a greengrocer. Another small shop that seems unique to Spain is one selling entirely frozen food (*alimentos congelados*) from open boxes. There are vegetables and also various types of fish, and frozen patties can be purchased in the quantities that suit you, for eating that day.

Specialist shops exist, of course. Spaniards are as fussy as the French about bread, which is bought fresh every day from *una panadería*. However this shop does not sell sweet breakfast rolls, pastries or cakes, which come from *una pastelería*. The latter may double up as *un salón de té*.

There are two types of ordinary butcher in Spain, and neither corresponds to our own. *La pollería* is a chicken shop, which basically sells chickens and eggs, but will probably include sausages and cheese as well. *Una carnecería* is a proper butcher, but will usually include a cold, cooked meat section (*una charcutería*).

Fish is bought in *una pescadería*, but buying it in a market is as common. Happily all these shop names are used for the counters in a supermarket too. In Cadiz, where the idea was invented, you may also find *una freíduria*, a take-away fried fish shop.

Supermarkets have come to Spain in a big way, and are particularly convenient when abroad, since a written price tag is easier to understand. Ask *¿Hay un supermercado por aquí?* – Is there a supermarket around here? Spanish supermarkets, however, still try to maintain a personal service. On meat and fish counters, food is usually cut and weighed to order. So a little Spanish, and a knowledge of what you want, is helpful.

Vast supermarkets, like the *hipermercado* and Pryca, are also worth a visit for their variety, although quantities may sometimes be too large to be practical. They are a good place to look at a massive display of local fish – all varieties, labelled and with prices – and to inspect *charcuterie* and local delicacies like pickled fish.

You will also find *una bombonería* (a sweet stall) in streets near schools, and in markets during local fairs. *Chumpas*, round lollipops on sticks, are popular.

THE SHOP OPENS AT. . . *(La tienda se abre a. . .)*

Shops are open six days a week, morning and evening, but closed for the afternoon *siesta*. This means evening shopping from 5–8 p.m. in most places, although some corner stores keep very late hours indeed, even opening briefly on Sunday. Normally *pastelerías* open for a couple of hours on Sunday morning – say 11–1 p.m. – and occasionally a local vegetable shop may follow suit.

Four weeks holiday is standard in Spain, and this is often taken all at once, so you may find shops *cerrado por vacaciones* in summer.

Protestant and northern visitors find closures for Saints days hard to anticipate. The days around Easter are obvious, but *Asunción* (the Feast of the Assumption) is on August 15, right in the middle of the main holiday season, and catches everyone out. The second Thursday after Whitsun – Corpus Christi – is another. If there is a Thursday closure for these, Spaniards *hacen un puente* ('make a bridge') and take Friday and Saturday as holidays too. Shops (and banks) close for a four-day run! The National day is St James – Santiago

Apostol – on July 25, celebrated particularly in Galicia.

Spanish holidays are also intensly regional. In the south many small villages will have two or three days of festival in August, traditionally a month with no agricultural work. Watch local posters for these. Every town and village also has its own saint for whom there will be celebrations – and local closures. The Virgin is widely celebrated, but on days that are purely local – like the Pilar festival in Zaragossa in October.

I WANT TO BUY. . . *(Quiero comprar. . .)*

If you know the Spanish word for what you want, but cannot see it, there are two extremely useful little words, both of them polite, that you can tack on in front. One is *¿Tiene?*, which means Do you have. . .? The other is *¿Hay?* Are there any. . .?

¿Tiene pan? Have you got bread? *¿Hay lechugas?* Are there any lettuces? And at the end of shopping, there will be the ritual question *¿Algo más?* Anything else?, to which you reply *Nada más*, Nothing else.

What does it cost?	*¿Cuánto costa?*
This one's cheaper	*Esto(a) es más barato(a)*
This one here	*Este aqui*
Bigger	*Más grande*
Smaller	*Más pequeño*
Give me. . .	*Déme. . .*
Go to the cash desk	*Pase por caja*

BREAD AND CAKE *(pan y pasteles)*

Bread is a basic of life, so important that the daily bread van still survives in some rural districts, visiting places that have no bakery. The day starts with bread. Twenty years ago it went into a bowl and the coffee and milk went in on top. Now crisp and fresh, perhaps with jam or honey, it accompanies coffee. Bread rolls, *panecillos* or *bollas*, are also called by names such as *chica* – a little girl – while you can get toast (*tostadas*) in town bars.

Bread is eaten fresh and white on the day it is made. Any leftover is used up another day, and the kitchen repertoire has lots of recipes for using up yesterday's loaf: at the bottom of soups or, crumbed and usually fried first, as a thickener in many famous sauces – extremely good when nuts and garlic are added too. Excellent garlic *croûtons* called *migas* are served with ham and eggs. Slices are also dipped in milk, then egg and fried. These *torrijas* are served to children at breakfast or tea-time. Bread and milk puddings (*pudíns*) are made too. Breadcrumbs are also much used in Spanish cooking; buy these ready-made, *pan rallado*.

In Galicia, which has its own way of doing things, dark rye bread (*pan de centeno*) is made in large loaves which may be divided for sale. A *pan de pagés*, a country loaf, is a very solid affair! Wholemeal bread is called *pan integral*. In the Basque country there is a flat bread called a *talo*.

Bread is part of every meal, replacing vegetables with the meat. Indeed the word for a slice, *rebanada*, comes from the verb to wipe round the plate. (In Spain it is positively bad manners to leave food on the plate.)

SWEET BREAD AND CAKES *(tortas y pasteles)*

Sweet breads and buns are sold at pastry shops. One attractive breakfast bread is simply called by the common name *torta*, an oval affair with sugar on top like a Bath bun. *Pan quemada*, Valencia's sweet bread, is glazed with egg white and sugar. *Suizos* are rolls with sugar in a hole – nothing to do with Swiss roll! More elaborate breads still are made for Christmas, in a ring, *roscon de Reyes*. In Mallorca and on the Barcelona coast a sweet roll called *ensaimada*, shaped like a snail's shell, is eaten for breakfast.

Pasteles (cakes) are eaten locally, although they do not compare well with French ones and were, in former times, made with lard. *La pastelería* will display a selection including cream-covered *gâteaux*, *turrón* and often quince jelly. Nothing is sold from the window display, which are samples and are very stale. The day's choice is under glass inside.

Puff pastry was probably invented in Spain by the Arabs, but the local version is rather heavy, although *millefeuilles* is widely made. My favourite is the plain *palmeras* or *delicia de hojaldre*, a copy of the French *palmier*. Heavy sweet pastries that keep well and resemble sponge cake are also popular. *Gâteau basque*, a two-layer tart filled with custard, is one such – excellent for picnics.

Cinnamon is the basic spice, going into everything sweet from biscuits, tarts and cakes to ice cream. Almonds are also much used. Sweets in a tradition dating back to Arab times are much the best, like *alfajores*, with honey and nuts in, or *polvorones*, so-called crumble cakes that melt in the mouth. *Mantecados* are dry cinnamon biscuit, for accompanying sweet wine. Many shapes are made, like *medias lunas*, half moons, or *mostachones*, in pairs of 'S's that look very like moustaches with pine-nuts on them.

Turrón is a candy dating to Arab times. There are two sorts: *jijona blando* is a soft coffee-coloured almond paste, while Alicante *turrón* is a hard white nougat, studded with almonds. *Pan de higos* is a fig, nut and chocolate mixture, set into a solid bar, rather like the Italian *panforte*. I have seen it stored with the *charcuterie*, where the chocolate will not melt. *Yemas* are still made by nuns, who obviously have a very sweet tooth, for these combine egg yolks (their name) with sugar, then are sugar coated. *Bocadillos de monja* are another nun's morsel, of almonds and sugar.

Frying-pan sweets are a tradition on the south and east coasts, an area with fewer ovens. Very good they are too, when freshly made, *churros* being the best known. The most sophisticated are *buñuelos de viento*, flyaway deep-fried choux puffs, and these will be filled with cream or custard. And there are rings of all sorts, called *rosquillos*.

GROCERIES *(comestibiles)*

You may be surprised to find some groceries labelled *ultramarinos*, meaning foreign goods. This is a survival from the times when foreign meant goods of a superior quality.

Coffee beans *(grano de cafe)* are universal while instant coffee is surprisingly expensive. **Teabags** of popular British brands are available everywhere. You will also see herb teas in several flavours, and bunches of camomile flowers on sale. **Chocolate** in Spain is still principally a drink. The powder is sold thickened and sweetened: just add hot milk. Spain is still not really into chocolate puddings or chocolate cakes and, although there are good chocolatiers in the Basque country, chocolate bars are generally of poor quality.

Jam *(mermelada)* in Spain is a well-cooked compote. This method is very successful for peaches *(melecotones)* and plum *(ciruelas)* but knocks the life out of berries. The favourite Spanish jam is made from a blotchy green pumpkin with stringy flesh called *cidra*, included in all the shop pastries. For orange marmalade, ask for *mermelada de naranja*.

Stewed dried **beans** *(judías o alubias secos)* and chickpeas *garbanzos*, are part of the Spanish way of life, but perhaps more welcome on a skiing holiday than in midsummer. Medium-grain **rice** has been cultivated in Spain since Arab times, although the most famous rice dish *(paella)* is only a couple of hundred years old. Cold rice salads are best made with long-grain rice. **Pasta** *(fideos)* is traditionally a short, thin vermicelli, although pasta is now sold in different grades and lasagne is easy to buy.

Oliva is the olive tree, rather than the fruit it bears, which is *aceituna*. **Olives** are often marinated by the individual grocer, who buys them after the first treatment. You will see a bowl on the end of the counter, with vinegar and spices in, and these cracked green olives will be a better buy than canned or bottled ones. Most **olive oil** *(aceite de oliva)* on sale in Spain is labelled 'pure' and is a mixture of virgin and refined oils. Spanish virgin oil is easier to buy abroad than it is in Spain. Since the Arabs promoted its use in the kitchen, olive oil has been much used for frying. It is a healthy fat, and also the safest fat for deep frying. A cheaper cooking oil is *aceite de girasol*, made from sunflower seeds.

Both red wine **vinegar** and also the more aromatic sherry vinegar (*vinaigre de Jerez*) are available. Use a little sherry vinegar to deglaze the pan after frying pork chops. It makes an excellent vinaigrette and is also the only vinegar to combine well with blue cheese.

Butter (*mantequilla*) is only a good buy in the north, for it quickly tastes off; use tubs of *margarina* instead.

Paprika is the basic **spice** in Spain, used to season before cooking, rather than as a garnish after it. The chillies that have so influenced Spanish cooking are sweet but mild – something few other cuisines can match. The red *choricero*, hung for drying in red *ristra* strings, gives the name and colour to *chorizo* sausages. Smallest and infinitely hot is the *guindilla*, sold dried or pickled. The Spanish meat palate is still very Arab, with cumin-flavoured sausages and cinnamon in many meat dishes. However, apart from paprika and black pepper, you can get by with coriander seeds (*culantro*), useful for cooked vegetables and meat. Spice mixes are also sold for barbecuing, like *pinchitos* (see MENUS AND RECIPES). But the quintessential Spanish spice is saffron, which gives the golden colour and perfume to *paella* and is a hidden presence in many fish soups and tomato-based sauces. For a dish for four use 20–25 stamens or 2g powder. (But be careful of the powdered varieties, since many are adulterated.)

The Spanish enjoy **salt cod** (*bacalao*). This is usually bought as a kite-shaped stiff board, salted split and without the head. It should not be yellow. Soak it for about 24 hours in a bowl of water, changing the water several times, then skin, debone and portion the fish. It doubles its weight when soaked, although this is lost again when skin and bones are removed. The result is not salty at all and can be cooked like fresh fish.

MILK, CHEESE AND EGGS
(leche, queso y huevos)

Milk is homogenized, which is sensible in a hot country. And it's also sold in UHT packs, which means it can be bought and kept. Will children like it? Probably not much, so look for flavoured milks – *batidos*. Milk is generally drunk far less in southern Europe, where temperatures are, on the whole, hot for cows and bad for milk storage. One big firm PULEVA (short for *pura leche vaca*) sells pasteurized milk, which makes a better cup of British tea. Cream is generally kept for young children, invalids – and desserts. Milk is normally bought in supermarkets, or in the small corner stores that offer bread, milk, jam, cans and bottles.

Ice cream (*helados*) is amazingly popular – and a long Spanish tradition. Every village has little shops with a freezer for lollies and ices. The normal flavours are sold – strawberry, lemon, vanilla and chocolate (*fresa, limón, vainilla y chocolate*) – but it's worth trying the unusual Spanish ones, like cinnamon (*canela*) and nougat (*turrón*). Unfortunately the quality of ice cream in inland Spain is poor – there is not enough fat in the cream – and you may find frozen fruit is a better bet. Even small shops may have frozen apples, pears or melons, puréed and stuffed back into the fruit skin. These are rock-hard and difficult to eat straight away, so might survive the journey back to your house or apartment. Remember to put them in the fridge for a while before eating them. Watch out for *horchata*, a milky drink, or an ice, sold in ice cream bars. Very creamy and sweet, it is made of ground tiger nuts. Yoghurt (*yogur*) is popular and sold everywhere in the usual flavours. Junket (*cuajada*) and fresh cream cheese are also eaten as dessert with honey or sugar.

Cheese is made all over the country, although more varieties are made in the north-west. Sheeps' and goats' milk cheeses outnumber the cows' milk ones, and they are mainly unpasteurized. Look for cheese in the market. You will get a choice of local products and also have a chance of buying fresh cheese. Manchego is the famous name, made from sheeps' milk. The drum-shapes may be covered in black or yellow wax, both marked with a rope pattern. Manchego is sold at various stages of ageing. Younger ones are softer and milder. Older ones are strong and crumbly.

I'd recognize Spanish hard cheese instantly, in any circumstances, in any part of the world. Anyone reared on it from childhood would find it a difficult addiction to shake off. The first one you try might be dull, or hard, or harsh, but it is worth finding a good one because they are genuinely a quality product. Smoking emphasizes the taste of traditional hard cheeses, like the Basque Idiazábal with its dark rind and San Simon, like an orange pear. Roncal is a Pyrenean cheese, drum-shaped with little rice-sized holes when mature. Mahón, from the Balearics, is square with an orange rind.

Cabrales is creamy blue cheese to challenge Roquefort, and is sold wrapped in maple leaves. Picón, made in the Picos de Europa, is very similar. Burgos is a soft ewes' milk cheese, a bit like *mozzarella*, available all over the country and used for dessert. The round Camerano comes from Rioja and is much more acidic. Puzol, on the Valencia coast, is round with a conical depression from the mould. The cows' milk Tetilla from Galicia is easily recognized by its breast-shape. Requesón is the general name for smooth cottage cheese; one popular Madrid version is called Miraflores.

Eggs are used lavishly in the Spanish kitchen. They are a formal course in a meal, are often used for coating, while hard-boiled eggs are much included in sauces to thicken them. Stuffed eggs with tuna were probably invented here too, while a garnish of eggs is common for salads. Eggs are also used to make two great Spanish sauces – mayonnaise, and the garlic and oil sauce *alioli* (which can also be made without eggs).

VEGETABLES *(legumbres)*

Those unfamiliar with Spanish food complain that it is greasy and drowned in **garlic**. But in fact, it is only raw garlic – and that from the garlic press – that is to be feared. The Spanish way is to cook it until mild. Spanish **onions** are a pleasant golden-bronze colour and are very mild, so that they can be eaten raw. Fried onion with garlic is the backbone of Spanish cooking. This is done very slowly, so they soften without catching or colouring and the sugar in them caramelizes slightly. Garlic is added at the end, so that it cannot brown. This *sofrito* often includes chopped parsley too, and chopped tomato is added as the next stage. This makes the base to soup, rice, sauce and stew.

Spaniards use the same word for vegetable **peppers** and for the condiment, like us. The familiar red and green ones are widely available. The *pimiento piquillo* – which means beak-shaped as it is long and pointed – is the Spanish choice for stuffing. It's spicier, crisper and has a thinner skin. These are also sold in jars, perfect for stuffing. There is also a small green pepper, used all over Spain for deep-frying whole.

The other peppers are what we would call **chillies**, for they are used for flavouring. Towards the end of summer you will see these hanging up to dry in strings. *Pimiento choricero* are used for flavouring all those red sausages. The hot chilli is *guindilla*, pronounced with a hard 'g', whose name means little cherry. It is dried and sold pickled.

Tomatoes were introduced to Spain as a vegetable to eat with peppers, and it was a long time before they were appreciated in their own right. **Aubergines** were introduced from Persia by the Arabs, and are mainly fried or stuffed. They are also often baked, when the flesh turns soft, then stuffed with rice and anchovies, ham or prawns, or tomato and cooked minced meat.

Spain was the first European country to get **potatoes**, although they have never replaced the chickpea as the basic starch. Spaniards have taken to *patatas fritas* in a big way. They are often fried, then added to a casserole or sauce, as in *patatas bravas* (see Chapter 8, MENUS AND RECIPES). They are also cooked in fish stews to absorb the liquid while eating.

Spinach is new in the south, possibly only thirty years old, but chard has been eaten for centuries and the old recipes for it are used for both. Cauliflowers, avocados, cabbages and lettuces are widely available. Artichokes are a pretty sight in the market; they are easiest cooked whole (see MENUS AND RECIPES). They are also often stripped to the base of edible flesh, and these are included in *paella* and vegetable stews. They make an interesting addition to potato salad, or eat them with mayonnaise and gherkins.

Mushrooms are hugely popular and Spaniards love to pick wild ones (*setas*) in the mountains. It is unwise to pick wild mushrooms in someone else's country, unless you are knowledgeable. Buy them from others who know what they are doing. In season the baskets appear in markets and La Boqueria in Barcelona has the most amazing selection. Wild mushrooms are usually cooked simply, with garlic and parsley, or are added to game casseroles.

I WANT TO BUY. . . *(Quiero comprar. . .)*

some	*unos, unas*
2lb (generous)	*un kilo*
1lb	*un medio, quinientos gramos*
½lb	*un quarto, doscientos cincuenta*
handful, bunch	*un manojo*

SALADS (ensaladas)

beetroot	*remolacha*
cucumber	*pepino*
fennel	*hinojo*
lettuce	*lechuga*
olives	*aceitunas*
parsley	*perejil*

pepper, green or red   *pimiento verde o rojo*
radishes   *rabanos*
spring onions   *cebolletas*
tomato   *tomate*
watercress   *berros*

VEGETABLES (legumbres)
artichokes (globe)   *alcachofa*
asparagus   *espárragos*
aubergine   *berenjena*
beans, broad   *habas*
beans, green   *judías verdes,*
cabbage, white (red)   *col blanco (lombardo)*
cabbage, green   *berza*
cauliflower   *coliflor*
chard   *acelga*
courgette   *calabacín*
leek   *puerro*
mushrooms, button   *champiñones*
mushrooms, wild   *setas, hongros*
onion   *cebolla*
peas   *guisantes*
potato   *patata*
pumpkin, squash   *calabaza*
spinach   *espinacas*
sweet potato (orange)   *batata (boniato)*

HERBS *(hierbas)*

It's not particularly easy to buy fresh herbs; the Spanish grow their own at home, because they wilt too quickly after cutting to make them marketable. If you stand a bunch in water it will last longer in the fridge, with a paper bag over the leaves.

Parsley (*perejil*) is flat-leaved with a mild taste. Tear the leaves off the stalk and add handfuls to salad. Chopped, it goes into the fried onion mixture *sofrito* (see VEGETABLES,

111

above) and is also combined with crushed bread and garlic in the *picada* (see MENUS AND RECIPES, Chapter 8) that is sprinkled over cooked fish, or used as a thickener for chicken sauce. The stalks have plenty of flavour, so crush them and add to stock for *paella*. If you get the barbecue going successfully, then dried rosemary and thyme are worth buying – or *hierbas para barbacoa*. But remember the hills around your holiday let are not as empty as they appear. Herb bushes flourish in the heat of the brown *sierras* – even lavender can be used. Throw the herbs on the barbecue as it dies down, or crumble the leaves onto fish or meat. Forget about measuring: do it in handfuls.

FRUIT *(fruta)*

Spain is the home of the **orange**, grown above all in Valencia. They favour navel oranges, although the Valencia orange remains the world's favourite. The area also grows tangerines and all the variations. You would think it would be easy to buy oranges, but this is not always so. In orange-growing parts – most of the south and east – everyone has a tree or a supplier, so oranges don't automatically go into the shops. **Lemons** *(limones)*, are the wonder fruit, for cooking and drinking. They grow by many kitchen doors and are always in season, since trees bear fruit and flowers simultaneously.

Fruit is seasonal and regional as well. Except in very sophisticated supermarkets, you won't find cherries or plums just because they are in season elsewhere. It's simply too hot to truck them around the country. **Apples** and **pears** are grown in most parts, while in the foothills of the Pyrenees there are great **peach** orchards, with fruit as big as oranges. **Cherries** grow in Almeria, around Granada and in Aragon, **plums** in the Rioja and **apricots** in warmer corners everywhere. Sweet **melons** *(melones)* are on sale throughout the year, especially the rugby-ball honeydews, with dark green or yellow skins. *Sandías*, large red-fleshed water melons, are mainly eaten as a slice in the hand – an instant drink, spitting out the seeds. The south and east coasts are famous for muscatel **grapes**.

It is also worth looking out for native fruit, which are valued less by the Spanish. Pomegranate bushes are used for hedging in the south. The fruit make a pretty addition to a salad, while the juice is used for cooking poultry. Cactuses grow on the harshest, rockiest land, and in midsummer produce **prickly pears** (*chumbos*), in a cheerful pink row along the top of each fleshy pad. Poor peasants sell them in markets. Prickly pears must be peeled with a glove and kitchen knife (or knife and fork), but are juicy and refreshing. Another wild fruit is **figs** (*higos*); early black ones are called *brevas*. **Loquats** (*nísperos*) are in season in late spring, an orange plum-shape, enclosing two or three dark stones, within a stiff skin. **Persimmons** (*caquis*) ripen around Christmas, a squashy, orange tree-tomato, spooned from its skin.

I WANT TO BUY. . . *(Quiero comprar. . .)*

some	*unos, unas*
2lb (generous)	*un kilo*
1lb	*un medio, quinientos gramos*
½lb	*un quarto, doscientos cincuenta*
handful, bunch	*un manojo*

FRUIT FOR PICNICS *(frutas para el campo)*

apple	*manzana*
apricots	*albaricoques*
banana	*plátano*
cherries	*cerezas*
dates, fresh	*dátiles*
figs (early black figs)	*higos (brevas)*
grapes, black or white	*uvas negras o blancas*
peach	*melocotón*
pear	*pera*
plums	*ciruelas*
tangerine	*tangerina*

water melon	*sandía*

MORE FRUIT *(fruta)*

custard apple	*anona, cherimoya*
figs in syrup	*higos en almíbar*
grapefruit	*pomelo*
lemon	*limón*
lime	*lima*
loquat	*níspero*
melon	*melón*
orange	*naranja*
peaches in syrup	*melocotones en almíbar*
persimmon	*caqui*
pineapple	*piña*
pomegranate	*granada*
prickly pear	*chumbo*
prunes	*ciruelas pasas*
raisins	*uvas pasas*
raspberries	*frambuesas*
strawberries	*fresas*

POULTRY AND GAME *(aves y caza)*

Spanish **chickens** *(pollos)* are a good buy and seem to have more flavour, even though they are battery-reared. You will find them in butchers, supermarkets and special chicken shops, which also sell eggs. Birds are sold fresh or frozen, portioned or whole. Ask for it *sin cabeza y patos*, without head or feet, *y limpiele, por favor*, and cleaned, please. One Spanish cut that I have not seen elsewhere is an escalope of breast *(escalopes de pechugas)* split with two cuts from inside, to open like a two-winged mirror, then flattened. It is fried like a veal escalope. Chicken giblets are eaten with eggs and rice, as are chicken livers *(higadillos)*.

Small **game birds** are part of the cuisine and a much better buy. You will see partridges *(perdices)* in cages, hanging on the wall outside a house, waiting until dinner time, while many small birds are still trapped or shot. *Coto de caza* ('private shooting') is a common sign in the extensive *sierras*. Quails (*codornices*) and pigeons or doves (*pichónes o palomas*) are easy to pot roast with wine and garlic. You can pick up the wings and legs if you can't manage to carve them neatly with knife and fork.

Rabbit (*conejo*) is very popular. Chopped, it is a basic ingredient for *paella* and is frequently stewed with garlic and onion, to which may be added *chorizo*, carrots, mushrooms, red wine, thyme and even chocolate – severally or all together.

MEAT AND CHARCUTERIE
(carne y charcuteria)

Butchers are not the medieval places they were twenty years ago, with unrecognizable lumps hanging on hooks. But even supermarkets still offer meat cut to order, rather than prepacked.

Lamb (*cordero*) is a luxury, grazed on numerous Spanish mountains in spring. It's an ideal meat for holidays – if you can get it – but expensive. **Beef** (*tenera*) is mainly reared in the north of the country and for this reason is often not a good buy in the south and east. However it is unlike our mature, hung beef. Animals are slaughtered at between one and two years – neither beef nor veal. Stewing beef comes from a cow (*carne de vaca*) or an ox (*carne de buey*). If you are on a skiing holiday, these make pleasant winter stews with wine and vegetables plus chestnuts, and in the east or south, fruit is traditional. If you are keen to avoid meat from the bullring – *la corrida* – you might like to know this is not legally sold in ordinary butchers. It's sold under special licence, often in municipal markets.

When shopping in the coastal resorts, judge from looking whether the meat has been supplied specially for you, the

115

tourist. If it has, it may well be cheaper than at home, and a bargain. To buy **steak**, simply ask for *biftek* or *entrecot de ternera* (our sirloin steak). The fillet is *un solomillo*, and normally is sold whole, while *chuletones*, wing rib chops, are enormous, a bone each is plenty. The roasting joints are topside (*lomo alta*) and sirloin (*lomo baja*).

Familiar **veal** cuts are available, like *chuletas de ternera*. Escalopes are often sold as *filetes* and I find *filetitos*, tiny ones which are the equivalent of Italian *scallopini*; they fry in seconds and are delicious with lemon juice or sherry over.

The universal meat, **pork** (*cerdo*) is sold everywhere. It has almost a religious symbolism in Spain, for eating it marked out the Christian after the Reconquest in 1492. Neither Muslims nor Jews were permitted pork. It is also the cheapest – and the countryside meat. Pork chops (*chuletas de cerdo*) are universal fare, fried or grilled with paprika and lemon juice. Tenderloin, (*solomillo*) makes a 20-minute roast, basted with orange juice or sherry, and loin off the bone (*lomo sin huesos*) is nearly as quick. Pork and veal are both used for stuffing vegetables and for making meatballs (*albóndigas*) and they can also be combined.

In the south *carne para pinchos*, ready-marinaded cubed pork (which looks yellowish, because of the cumin) is sold for kebabs (*pinchos*) (see Chapter 8, MENUS AND RECIPES). *Tocino* is fat pork belly, sometimes raw, but usually salt. Slices are cut from this, then cubed and fried as the base of many vegetable dishes. The word is sometimes still used for bacon rashers (same bit of the pig, but necessarily leaner) but the word bacon (*beicón*) is now often used for a rasher. *Pancetta* is cured pork flank, a belly cut and like our streaky bacon, except that it is rolled. Cold, cooked pork loin is *lomo cocido* or *adobado*. *Pudín de cerdo* is like corned beef, except that it's made of pork, pressed shreds gelled together with a little fat.

Chorizos are Spain's scarlet **sausage**, ready for frying whole, sliced or grilling. A common country affair 'with the tomato ketchup already in them', they are flavoured with paprika.

The hot ones are tied with red string, or have red metal links. Home-made ones are *a la casera.* Many sausages (*salchichas*) are traditionally used in long-stewed dishes, in Spain's famous boiled *cocidos* for example, and in bean dishes. There are many regional varieties. On the east coast you will find *butifarras*, a greyish-white fat sausage made from veal and pork, for frying in slices with fresh beans. The best come from the town of Vich.

Types of sausage that don't require cooking include a larger *chorizo* (about 5 cm [2 in] across) which is sliced diagonally. *Salchichon* is the Spanish version of *salami*, though the Italian original – and *mortadella* – are also on sale. There is also a sweet black *morcilla dulce*, with cinnamon. *Sobresada* is a speciality of Catalonia, found in Mallorca and Barcelona. It is a red, raw sausage, so soft that it is often served in pots, without its skin. A rather similar paprika-pork fat paste, found in the south, is *mantecado colorado*. Both are spread on bread.

Raw ham (*jamón serrano*) is Spain's glory, frequently eaten as *tapas* (see Chapter 6, EATING AND DRINKING). On average, Spaniards consume a ham each every year and this is largely in small quantities in cooking. Lesser ones are cured off the bone and are sold from the cold cabinet. Cooked ham on the bone is called *jamón de york* and is carved to order. Occasionally there are also *salones* on sale, cured meat that may be lamb or beef. Moulded cooked hams, *fiambre de paleta* or *fiambre de magro*, which means pressed lean meat, are cheaper.

I WANT TO BUY. . . *(Quiero comprar. . .)*

beef	*ternera, carne de buey*
chops	*chuletas*
cut across in steaks	*en filetes al través*
fillet steak	*solomillo*
in four slices	*en cuatro lonjas*
kebab cubes	*carne para pinchos*
lamb	*cordero*

117

lean meat (ham)	*magro*
loin	*lomo*
mince	*carne picada*
one slab of meat	*una pedazo de carne*
pork	*cerdo*
rib beefsteak (on bone)	*chuletón*
roasting, suitable for	*asadero*
sliced diagonally	*en tajadas*
steak	*biftek, entrecot*
without bones	*sin huesos*

FISH AND SHELLFISH *(pescados y mariscos)*

The selection of fresh fish is wonderful and at the same time bewildering. What are their names and how do you cook them? Are there difficult bones that will put children off eating them? Soup-stews are an easy way to eat fish while avoiding the bones: the carcasses go in first to make soup and are then strained out. Vegetables and fillets go in next and are sent to table.

To ask for fish to be cleaned: *Limpielo, por favor*. Ask for steaks: *Cortelo al través*, or for fillets: *En filetes a lo largo*. I want to take the bones and heads is: *Déme las cabezas y huesos*.

Tuna have impressive, submarine-shaped bodies, without scales. Good barbecue steaks are taken from across the tail. *Bonito*, the pretty tuna (canned as skipjack), is popular in the north of Spain and this one is marked with black bars radiating backwards. The *atún blanco* is the long-finned *albacora*, rarer in the Mediterranean than the Atlantic. The *bacoreta* has scribblings on its back. All are good well marinated then barbecued. The blue-fin tuna (*atún*) is more of a problem, with dark-fleshed steaks, like bloody horsemeat. The best bit is the belly flaps (*ventresca*), like flank steak. Marinate it, put in a pot, heap with vegetables and casserole slowly with wine. **Swordfish** (*pez espada*) will almost certainly have the proud head displayed, with its black sword.

Sardines (*sardinas*) are particularly prized on the north coast, where they have their own festival. One method of barbecuing is to run a stick down through half a dozen, like a square-rigged mast, and grill beside a beach fire. They are also casseroled with tomato. Small fresh anchovies are black-backed and seem very slim compared with the stubbier silver sardines. These are fried, or marinated raw, then served with vinaigrette.

Grill **red mullet** (*salmonetes*) without bothering to clean inside – fry or pickle them. Another small fish is *pescadillo*, silver hake, used for soup and frying, for the fillets come off the backbone with one cut of the knife (see hake below). **Sole** (*lenguada*) are often fished small (buy one or more per person) and like *gallo*, a similar flat fish, are fried and served with plenty of lemon. **Plaice** (*platija*) are good when available.

A fish weighing a kilo or so can be filleted or grilled, but often ends up baked whole with wine. **Bream** is a good candidate for this treatment. *Dorada* is the best of them and is called the 'gilt-head', because of its distinctive yellow eyebrow on a pinkish-gold fish. *Besugo* is 'red' bream, but is more pinkish-grey, with a black spot on the shoulder. *Denton* is another bream, also with reddish tints. The latter pair are often grilled. Ray's bream (*palometa negra*) a roundish brown-grey fish with a large eye, has excellent fillets.

Lubina is **sea bass**, one of finest fish available, with trouble-free bones. It is silver with a darker back and white belly. **Grey mullet** – the best is *lisa*, with distinctive front-to-back grey stripes, but *mújol* is also good – are a useful size. They need careful cleaning, as the bellies are often full of grey sand.

I believe Spain started the present fashion for **monkfish** (*rape*), called *pixín* in the north. The Spanish preference, however, is for **hake** (*merluza*), a dark-grey fish with a tubular body. The ribs are unusually solid, the backbone rising upwards like the breastbone of a chicken, so the fillets come off, one either side, in solid, round chunks of perfect meat. Cut the belly flaps off and use separately; the belly is lined with a black skin which must be removed.

119

Mero, translated as **grouper**, is much squatter in profile, reddish with faint grey 'cloud shadows' on its back and generously finned. The flesh is flaky and delicious. The **John Dory** (*Pez de San Pedro*) is rounder still and flatter, easily recognizable by the black thumb print on either side, where St Peter lifted it from the water. It is fine-flavoured and structured like a plaice, with flesh that separates easily into four bone-free fillets, which make up only about a third of its total weight.

Raya is the more familiar **skate**, and only the triangular wings are sold. After cooking the flesh falls easily from the bones. It is commonly fried, with an acid addition like capers (*alcaparras*).

Salmon (*salmón*) swim up rivers into the Picos de Europa in the north. Demand, however, is so great that they are also imported from Norway. The rivers in Asturias and the Pyrenees are also full of brown **trout**, like the *truchas de Bierzo*. However, more common are farmed, rainbow trout. These are commonly fried, grilled or poached in red or white wine; a characteristic partnership is with raw ham, both of them fried in the same fat.

Aguja is the **gar** or needle fish, with a nose like a knitting needle. It grills and casseroles well. Some people are put off by the backbone, which turns bright green when cooked, but it doesn't affect the taste. **Mackerel** (*caballa*) is an oily fish, so it grills well. In Spain it is cooked with peppers and chillies, and recipes often have potato in, to absorb some of the fat.

Any fish without its skin and looking like a meat bone will be shark, peeled to the pink flesh and generally called *rosada*.

SHELLFISH *(mariscos y crustácea)*

Shellfish are sold raw and will always be a more expensive purchase, although prices are cheaper than at home – despite the fact that a lot of British shellfish end up in Spain.

Deep-water **prawns** (*langostinos*) are a better buy than the equally large, scarlet *carabineros*, which owe their name to the military colour of their uniforms. *Gambas* and *quisquilla* are

both names of our common prawn, while *cigales* is what the Italians call *scampi*. All these shellfish need cooking. Ten minutes in boiling water for the big ones, down to about three or four minutes for little prawns.

The true **lobster** (*bogovante*) is rare and *langosta*, the spiny rock lobster without visible claws, is preferred. This is boiled for 20 minutes or so, depending on size, to eat with mayonnaise, and can also be split and grilled on a barbecue.

Crabs range from *nécoras*, which are small shore crabs, served just boiled, a couple to a portion, to pick clean or put into soups, to *cangrejo*, with the monster claws. A favourite, particularly on the north coast, is *centolla*, called *txangurro* in the Basque country. This is the knobbly-shelled spider crab, with claws that hardly feature. The flesh is stronger than normal crabs, so is often combined with a little hake.

Fiddly, tiny shellfish, like tiny raw **clams** (*almejas o coquinas*) or tiny prawns (*camarones*) on the south coast, are best picked at, with sherry, over a lazy lunch. Rinse them well in water with plenty of salt. They can also be added to sauces or soups – cockles (*beberechos*) are best done this way too – when they will save you trouble by opening themselves. Larger clams, like the *concha fina*, which has a fine mahogony-coloured Venus shell, need opening with a sharp knife shoved in at the side of the back joint. It reveals a glory of scarlet and orange, hence the name, and is best eaten raw, with a glass of cool *fino*. *Navajos*, razor shells (long and brown), are best steamed.

Mussels (*mejillones*) are steamed open after careful washing (see p. 158 in MENUS AND RECIPES) and can then be served with lemon or a vinaigrette, hot or cold, or go into rice and pasta dishes or a score of fish soups. Some of the biggest and best are farmed in the Atlantic bays of Galicia. **Scallops** are also famed in this part of the world, called *vieras* or *conchas pelegrinas*, since the shell was the badge of pilgrims to Santiago. Rinse and remove the gristly surround, then fry or poach the flesh briefly, or grill on the flat shell on a barbecue till the flesh is opaque.

True **oysters** (*ostras*) are rare. *Ostiones*, the meaty Portuguese oysters, edible throughout the summer, have largely replaced them. These are breadcrumbed for fritters, or grilled briefly.

Pulpo is **octopus** and you are more likely to eat this out than cook it yourself. But **squid** (*calamares*) are easy. Cleaning is described in Chapter 8, MENUS AND RECIPES. Cut into rings, these are deep-fried in batter, or can be briefly fried with onion, peppers and garlic and added to cooked *fideos*. They are a major constituent of soups and fish stews. Cuttlefish (*sepia*, or *jibia*) can be grilled if small. It is cleaned almost identically, except that a slit is needed to extract the porous white bone. The meat is sweeter but tougher than squid, so they often end up cubed and braised in stews with tomato or other vegetables, or stuffed with rice, then braised.

WINE AND DRINKS *(vino y bebidas)*

For practical reasons much bottled wine is bought in supermarkets, but virtually every grocery store sells alcohol. It is also legal to consume alcohol almost anywhere, including in the street.

Look out for wine cellars. These *bodegas* sometimes have barrels piled to the ceiling and offer fortified wines on tap. As these are usually from the local vineyards, this is a good way to try out local products. Bring your own bottles (sherry bottles with corks are ideal), sample first and then fill.

A word of warning. The modern French-style Spanish white wines (see Chapter 6, EATING AND DRINKING) are not much good for cooking. The very lightness that makes them agreeable for drinking means that they lack staying power. Use a good-quality white Rioja *blanco* or an *alberiño* for fish. A cheaper alternative is white vermouth (*vermú seco*). Sherry is also good, the dry *fino* from Montilla, or medium-dry *amontillado*. Whenever a few tablespoons of stock are needed – when the tomatoes in a sauce look like drying out, or in the frying pan after cooking veal – add a splash of sherry.

CHAPTER EIGHT

MENUS AND RECIPES

You'll almost certainly want to try the local produce and regional dishes. However, if you're not familiar with the area, it can be difficult to find out what's on offer. Even when you do stumble across something you like, what ingredients do you need? What other dishes go well with it? And how long does it take to prepare? Even the most enthusiastic self-caterers don't want to spend hours and hours in the kitchen – after all, this is a holiday!

The menus and recipes given here vary from the quick-and-simple to those with the more adventurous cook in mind, and the ingredients are easily obtainable. Some menus take into account that there will be evenings when no one feels like cooking and rely on items which, while being distinctively Spanish, can be bought at a supermarket, grocer's or pastry shop, and require almost no preparation.

The ingredients are listed with their Spanish translations and the odd brand name, so that you know what to ask for or look for when you shop. Where the ingredient is something you will be buying specifically for the dish, such as '4 thin slices of raw ham' it is translated precisely, including quantities 'cuatro tajadas ligeras de serrano'. However, where the item is something you are likely to buy anyway, only its name is translated – so '1 garlic clove, finely chopped' is simply translated as 'ajo' (garlic).

NOTE ON MEASUREMENTS

The metric measurements are converted into imperial, but as a rough guide, 1 kilogram = just over 2lb, while 100 grams = about 4oz. However, measurements in holiday recipes are not crucial – and your holiday kitchen may well have no scales. I have occasionally translated a weight into a volume measure, giving rice or sugar in cups as well, to help if you are forced to guess. My teacup is a little under half a pint.

The only crucial measurement is rice: 2 cups make *paella* for 4 people, and 1 cup of rice feeds 4 as a side dish. And to cook Spanish rice, you need a little more than double its volume – 2¼ cups of liquid per cup of rice.

LIGHT MEALS

The first of these is the Spanish sandwich, and therefore picnic-possible. The second is also made of bread, but is really a do-it-yourself bread salad. It's least messy on a plate, but is perfectly possible to make by the pool.

BOCADILLOS

Spanish sandwiches

For a good *bocadillo*, buy long, fresh, crusty loaves, a good 20cm (8in) per person, or big rolls. Where I live in the south, these are called *chicas* – little girls. Split them and spread each side with olive oil – far nicer than butter, which so easily goes rancid in the course of a morning walking. Thin slices of raw ham (*serrano*) carved from the bone and hard cheese of the Manchego type are the classic fillings – 50g (2oz) a head of each is generous. With a bag of olives and an orange each, this makes a splendid picnic.

Tomato with slices of the bigger *chorizo para comer crudo*, to eat raw, also make a good filling, though messier. If the *bocadillos* are being eaten at once, I like mussels in a little tomato sauce (see recipe for mussel soup). Or simply steam open a kilo (2lb), shell them and stuff into the bread, with a little chopped onion. I think they might be a health risk if they are carried in the heat for any length of time.

PA AMB TOMAQUET

Catalan tomato bread

Pa amb tomáquet means tomato bread, and this is eaten with most Catalan meals – salad or otherwise. Cut the bread across into rounds, and toast very lightly indeed. Give everyone a half tomato, and squish the juice into the bread on both sides. Then dribble a teaspoon of good olive oil on each side. I like the bread wiped with a cut garlic clove too. Slices of *serrano* and/or cheese are a common topping.

ENTREMES DE CARNE Y LEGUMBRES

Cold meat and cooked vegetable salad

For a really quick lunch there is always the cold-meat counter (*una chacinería o charcutería*). Cold meats are *los fiambres*. The cheaper things on it are also bland: like roast turkey breast (*pavo solo*); pressed ham (*fiambre de magro de cerdo*); cooked pork (*lomo cocido*); pressed tongue (*fiambre de lengua*); or anything made of pressed, minced meat, described in Spain as *chopped*, such as *chopped de ternera* – minced veal loaf. You will also find familiar Italian sausages, such as *mortadella*.

For four people ask for 4 slices (*Quisiera comprar cuatro tajadas*), and ask for it bigger (*mas grande*), or smaller (*mas pequeño*), when the assistant waves her knife.

Canned marinaded vegetables make a lively accompaniment. I am particularly fond of *berenjenas aliñados*, which are small aubergines the size of plums in a spicy tomato dressing. Other cooked vegetables in tomato sauce, similar to ratatouille, are *samfaina*, which contains aubergine, and *pisto*, without it.

PIPIRRANA CON SERRANO

Chopped pepper and cucumber salad with raw ham

This salad comes from Jaén near Granada. It is Arab in origin, eaten well chilled and so is close to being gazpacho. Chilled soups, however, need a blender and furnished apartments rarely have them.

2 small green peppers, without seeds	*dos pimientos verdes*
2 fat tomatoes, skinned	*tomates*
1 cucumber, from the fridge	*pepino*
2 tablespoons chopped Spanish onion	*cebolla*
1 garlic clove, finely chopped	*ajo*
1 teaspoon salt	*sal*
1 tablespoon vinegar	*vinagre*
2 tablespoons olive oil	*aceite de oliva*
black pepper	*pimienta*
flat parsley leaves (optional)	*perejil*
4 thin slices raw ham	*cuatro tajadas ligeras de serrano*

Quarter the peppers and remove any white ribs. Cut into long thin shreds (double matchstick width) and then into neat dice. With a sharp knife take out the insides of the tomatoes, discard seeds and juice and dice the flesh. Peel the cucumber, split it and use a teaspoon to remove and discard the seeds. Dice like the rest and put them all in a bowl.

Chop the garlic finely, then use the flat of a table knife to crush it. Sprinkle with salt, then work the garlic to a paste. Move to a cup and add the oil and vinegar. Dress the salad, adding a little pepper, and chill for 30 minutes before serving. Flat parsley leaves make a nice addition. Serve with the *serrano. (Serves 4)*

PINCHOS

Cumin pork kebabs

*In the south of Spain cubed pork is on sale ready-marinaded
for this popular dish. You can tell it by its yellowish hue.
If it is not, the marinade powder for it is sold ready-mixed
in groceries and supermarkets in the spice section,
(las especias). It's simply labelled 'pinchitos'.
Before you buy the meat check that you have a working
grill. Barbecuing over charcoal is so common that it by no
means follows that your oven has a top grill, or that it
works. You may also need to buy skewers (agujas para
pinchos). If you do have a barbecue and can find wild
rosemary or other bushy herbs while out walking, try putting
a few bunches on the hot coals.*

800g (1¾lb) ready-trimmed
marinaded pork cubes
6 tablespoons olive oil

*ochocientos gramos de
cerdo para pinchos
aceite de oliva*

If you are using ready-mixed marinade powder, sprinkle the
meat with olive oil and then half the packet spices. Rub in
with your hands and leave for an hour.

Smear the kebabs with oil and give them 20 minutes under
or over the heat, turning regularly. A simple salad of lettuce,
sliced tomato and onion, with a handful of olives on top,
makes a good accompaniment. *(Serves 4)*

GAMBAS CON MAHONESA Y ALCAPARRAS

Freshly cooked prawns with caper mayonnaise

Prawns, shrimps and scampi (cigales) are all sold semi-raw. There is a lot of choice: the large prawns (langostinos), the more familiar prawn (gambas or sometimes quisquilla), and the tiny shrimps (camarones). You will get 10–12 cigales in a kilo (2lb) if they are sold with the heads, and this will be an expensive purchase. Half a kilo (1lb) of small prawns is quite enough for four. They are wonderful freshly boiled and served with mayonnaise. Capers grow on all the mountains overlooking the Mediterranean and make a nice acid addition. Freshly made potato salad and iced beer make this a perfect lunch in hot weather.

500g–1kg (1–2lb) prawns or scampi	*un medio kilo/un kilo de gambas/cigales*
salt	*sal*
2–3 tablespoons capers	*alcaparras*
150g (5fl oz) mayonnaise	*un tarro de mahonesa*

Bring a large pan of salted water to the boil and throw in the shellfish, in two batches if you bought a kilo. A big scampi with its head will need 8–10 minutes. *Langostinos* need 5–6 minutes and *gambas* 3–4 minutes. Cook shrimps in batches – just in and out for a minute. Drain and serve in a big dish, scattered with coarse salt if you have it.

Crush the capers with the back of a spoon, stir into the mayonnaise and pile in a bowl. Provide extra plates, and serviettes for the shells if they are still hot. Serve with bread or potato salad. *(Serves 4)*

ENSALADA CATALANA

Catalan salad

*This is one of many combined salads made in the Pyrenees.
Finely shredded cabbage can replace the lettuce: red is
lombardo, a white head is un col blanco. Judge the sausages
by their size – some white butifarras are quite large. You
might also find smaller black ones.*

6–8 tablespoons olive oil	*aceite de oliva*
275g (10oz) potatoes, diced	*patatas*
50g (2oz) raw ham, diced	*cincuenta gramos de serrano*
2 spicy sausages	*dos chorizos, morcillas or butiffaras*
50g (2oz) hazelnuts	*avellanas*
1 lettuce	*lechuga*
salt, black pepper	*sal, pimienta*
2 tablespoons wine vinegar	*vinagre*

Heat the oil in a small *paella* pan and when it is very hot, put
in the potatoes. Fry for 5 minutes over high heat, turning
until they are sealed on all sides. Turn down the heat and
cook the potatoes through, stirring occasionally – about 20
minutes. Add the diced ham and the thinly sliced sausages for
the last 10 minutes, turning them occasionally.

Hazelnuts are easiest to toast in a low oven in a tray for 20
minutes, shaking every now and then, but can be dry-fried, if
you shake the pan every half minute.

Prepare the lettuce and arrange on 4 plates.

When the potatoes, ham and sausage are cooked, season
with salt and pepper and spoon into the middle of the lettuce,
distributing the sausage slices fairly. Pour the vinegar into the
pan and bring to the boil, scraping round the pan. Pour the
hot dressing over the lettuce on the four plates, sprinkle with
crushed hazelnuts and serve at once. Good with cold beer.
(Serves 4)

THE MAIN MEAL (*LA COMIDA*)

Pepper salad with anchovies
Ham and potato omelette
Orange salad with caramel syrup

PIMIENTOS CON ANCHOAS

Pepper salad with anchovies

If you're in a hurry, use two cans of peppers (dos latas de pimientos morrones). However, grilled fresh vegetables are much sweeter and juicer – and a basic of Spanish cooking. I always grill them if I am serving this salad with hard-boiled eggs as the main course.

3 red peppers   *tres pimientos rojos*
2 × 50g (2oz) cans anchovies   *dos latas de anchoas*

Grill the peppers for about 20 minutes, giving them a quarter turn every 5 minutes, until they are charred on all sides. Alternatively, bake them in a hot oven for the same time, turning once.

Put them in a plastic bag (*un bolsa de plástico*) for 10 minutes, then move to a plate (to catch the sweet juice). Strip off the charred skins and pull out the stalks and seeds. Open them, remove the last seeds and cut into strips.

Decorate with a criss-cross of anchovies. Sprinkle with a little oil from the can and serve with crusty bread. (*Serves 4*)

TORTILLA DE SERRANO Y PATATES

Spanish ham and potato omelette

Spanish omelettes are like cakes, cut into solid wedges, not creamy and flat, like French ones. Cooked sausage, prawns and fried onions are other good fillers. Buy serrano for cooking en un lonja (in a thick slice) – from the chilled cabinet, not the tapas grade on the bone. Serve tortillas hot, warm or cold. They make a substantial sandwich filler (see bocadillos, page 126) and chunks are good reheated in tomato sauce.

125ml (4fl oz) olive oil	*aceite de oliva*
100g (4oz) raw ham,	*cien gramos de serrano*
or 2 *chorizos*, diced	*o dos chorizos*
½ large red pepper, diced	*pimiento rojo*
500g (1lb) potatoes, diced	*patatas*
6 large eggs	*seis huevos grandes*
salt, black pepper	*sal, pimienta*

Heat a small *paella* pan, about 23cm (9in), with a generous quantity of oil until very hot, add the diced ham or *chorizos* and sauté quickly with the chopped pepper; the *chorizo* should be coloured on all sides. Remove from the pan to a bowl lined with kitchen paper. Add the potatoes to the pan and stir. Reduce the heat and let the potatoes cook through, which takes about 15 minutes, turning them over frequently so they do not colour. Remove to the bowl.

Drain the oil from the pan into a cup and wipe out the pan with paper if there are any sticky or crusty patches. Strain about 2 tablespoons oil back into the pan, and reheat. Beat the eggs together and season them well with salt and pepper. Pull the paper from under the potatoes and pour the eggs over them, so they are well coated. Pour the mixture into the hot oil, distributing everything evenly, and give it a minute at high heat to set, before turning down the heat. Use a spatula to pull the *tortilla* off the sides of the pan to make an upright edge, shaking the pan to and fro occasionally, to make sure the bottom isn't catching.

When the top has ceased to be liquid, cover with a serving plate and reverse the pan to turn the *tortilla* out. Add 2 more tablespoons of oil, return the *tortilla* to the pan cooked side up – and cook for a further 2–3 minutes. Serve hot. Green salad goes well with it. *(Serves 4)*

NARANJAS ACARAMELIZADOS

Orange salad with caramel syrup

An old Spanish way of serving oranges. Ten minutes in the freezer makes them easier to slice neatly.

300g (10oz) sugar	*azúcar*
300ml (10fl oz) water	
6 oranges	*seis naranjas*
toasted almonds (optional)	*almendras tostadas*

Put the sugar (about ¾ cup) and 125ml (4fl oz) water in a saucepan. Stir until it begins to boil, then boil gently for 10 minutes till it is a rich golden colour. Standing well back, add 175ml (6fl oz) boiling water – be careful because it splatters. Stir to dissolve.

Peel the oranges, taking off the outside membrane too, and slice. Arrange in a bowl and pour the syrup over. Toasted crushed almonds are nice on top, if you have them. *(Serves 4)*

Globe artichokes with vinaigrette
Individual baked fish dishes
Fruit

ALCACHOFAS CON VINAGRETA

Globe artichokes with vinaigrette

Fine-looking globe artichokes are continental food, best eaten warm, or barely cold. All the work is done at the table. To make a salad lunch, remove the chokes and stuff the centres too: mayonnaise, chopped eggs and pickles, or canned tuna, or canned vegetable salads like samfaina and pisto, or left-over fish with its sauce all make good fillings.

4 large globe artichokes	*cuatro alcachofas*
125ml (4fl oz) olive oil	*aceite de oliva*
3 tablespoons vinegar	*vinagre*
salt, black pepper	*sal, pimienta*

Remove the stalks from the artichokes by snapping them off; this will bring away most of the stringy fibres underneath. Trim the bottom almost flat. If they are very stringy, they will need 40 minutes cooking. Otherwise allow about 20 minutes. Put them in a large pan, add water and salt and bring to the boil, uncovered, then time them as they cook. Drain them upside down for 10 minutes to cool a little.

Lay a spare plate for discarded leaves and give each person a little dish of vinaigrette, mixing the remaining ingredients.

If you have never eaten artichokes before, pull off a few leaves and dip the pad of flesh at the back into the vinaigrette, then pull this off with your teeth, discarding the leaf. When you near the middle – the leaves make a soft, lighter cone – pull this off whole. Underneath is the bristly choke. Ease it out with a knife and discard. Then put the base into your vinaigrette pot, cut it up and eat it. *(Serves 4)*

CAZUELITAS DE PESCADO

Individual baked fish dishes

Most Spanish kitchen cupboards have sets of brown dishes, glazed on the inside only for cooking. Cazuelitas, little ones, 15cm (5½in) across, are ideal for baking one-person dishes. In the north, this dish might be made with salmon and dry cider, but elsewhere it is more likely to be hake (merluza), which is Spain's most popular fish or, in the Mediterranean, the splendid mero, which is grouper. The word for a fish steak and a fish fillet are the same in Spanish – filete – so you must ask for the fish en filetes a lo largo – what we call fillets – or al través en filetes, cut across into steaks, according to the size and shape of the fish.

The best shellfish for a sauce are those that trap seawater within two shells (mussels, cockles and clams). But 100g (4oz) prawns – cien gramos de gambas – make a colourful substitute, as do a handful of frozen peas. A little grated cheese can be substituted for the shellfish, but parsley is essential.

1 Spanish onion, chopped	*cebolla*
1 garlic clove, finely chopped	*ajo*
3 tablespoons olive oil	*aceite de oliva*
4 fish steaks or fillets, 150–175g (5–6oz) each	*cuatro filetes de pescado, ciento cincuenta gramos la cada*
salt, black pepper	*sal, pimienta*
½ lemon	*limón*
1 tablespoon flour	*harina*
200g (7oz) clams or mussels, or a mix	*doscientos gramos de almejas or mejillones*
100g (4oz) grated potato	*patate*
200ml (7fl oz) fish stock, (page 151 or could be made with a cube)	*cubos de caldo de pescado*
200ml (7fl oz) white Rioja or dry vermouth	*Rioja blanco o vermú seco*
4 tablespoons chopped parsley	*perejil*

Heat the oil in a large *paella* pan and fry the onion over low heat until soft, then add the garlic. Heat the oven to high if butane gas (200 C, 400 F, gas 6, if there is a regulator). Pour a little oil into four *cazuelitas* and rub round the inside.

Season the fish pieces with salt and pepper and sprinkle with lemon juice. Rinse clams or clean the mussels (page 158). Prepare the potato and heat the stock and wine together.

Push the onion to the sides of the pan. Flour the fish lightly and fry on both sides briefly over high heat.

Transfer both to the *cazuelitas*, skin side down if fillets. Surround the fish with grated potato and sprinkle with parsley. Season and add the wine and stock and any leftover lemon juice. Distribute the shellfish round the fish. Bake for 15–20 minutes, when the clams or mussels will open. Serve with bread and a green salad. *(Serves 4)*

> White asparagus with two sauces
> Chicken Santander
> Junket or cream cheese with honey, or yoghurt

This is a northern menu. The starter is from Rioja, where the best white asparagus are grown, and canned to send around the country. This is followed by a typically Spanish chicken and rice dish, and a creamy bought dessert ends the meal.

ESPARRAGOS CON DOS SALSAS

White asparagus with two sauces

Canned asparagus are huge, white and fleshy: a luxury at half the price it would be at home. Allow 4–5 spears per person: this works out at 2 small cans, or one big one, or a jar. Increase the quantity by at least half if you have this as a salad lunch, and serve with egg salad or mayonnaise instead of vinaigrette.

400g (14oz) canned asparagus (minimum 16 spears)	*una lata de cuatrocientos gramos de espárragos*
VINAIGRETTE	
125ml (4oz) olive oil	*aceite de oliva*
3 tablespoons vinegar	*vinagre*
salt, black pepper	*sal, pimienta*
RAW TOMATO SAUCE	
1–2 ripe tomatoes	*tomates maduros*
1 tablespoon chopped Spanish onion	*cebolla*
1 tablespoon chopped parsley (optional)	*perejil*
cayenne	*pimentón picante*

Drain the asparagus well and put it on a dish.
Mix the vinaigrette ingredients together in a jug.

Skin the tomatoes – they should peel easily. If not, quarter them, and remove the skin with a knife. Discard the seeds and juice and chop the flesh in neat dice. Mix in the onion and parsley (if you can get it) and season lightly with salt and cayenne. Arrange in neat piles round the asparagus, and pass the vinaigrette. Eat the asparagus first with one sauce, then the other. *(Serves 4)*

POLLO CAMPURRIANO

Chicken Santander

*The chicken is cooked with wine and served with rice. It is
made with supermarket ingredients. Frying chicken in
paprika is the classic Spanish method.*

6 tablespoons olive oil	*aceite de oliva*
1 Spanish onion, chopped	*cebolla*
salt, pepper	*sal, pimienta*
4 small chicken quarters,	*cuatro cuartos*
1.2kg (2lb 8oz) altogether	*de pollo, aproximadamente un kilo y cuarto*
3 teaspoons paprika	*pimentón dulce*
2 teaspoons flour	*harina*
150g (5oz) raw ham, cubed	*ciento cincuento gramos de serrano*
2 peppers, green and red, chopped	*dos pimientos, rojo y verde*
2 garlic cloves, finely chopped	*ajo*
8 fat white spring onion heads, 3–4 green tops chopped	*cebollones o cebolletas*
1 bay leaf	*hoja de laurel*
500ml (16oz) chicken stock, made with a cube	*cubos de caldo de pollo*
200g (7oz) medium-grain rice (1 cup if you have no scales) rinsed in a colander	*arroz*
250ml (8oz) white wine	*vino blanco*

Start by heating 4 tablespoons oil in a small *paella* pan and
put the chopped onion over low heat to soften. Salt and
pepper the chicken well, rubbing with 2 teaspoons paprika,
then dust with flour.

When the onion is half done, increase the heat and add the
chicken pieces, skin down. Fry for 5 minutes on each side.

Meanwhile start another casserole in which the chicken will fit tightly in one layer. Add 2 tablespoons oil and fry the chopped *serrano* and peppers, with 1 chopped garlic clove.

When the chicken is golden, tip the ham and peppers out of the second pan and put them aside. Pack the chicken in neatly with the spring onion bulbs in the spaces. Sprinkle with remaining flour and tuck in the bay leaf. Pack the ham and peppers back on top, pushing them down between the chicken pieces. Add 250ml (8oz) chicken stock and cover with a lid.

Add the second chopped garlic clove and the rice to the onion over a low heat. Sprinkle with 1 teaspoon paprika and stir gently. Pour in the wine and bring gently to the boil. Add the rest of the stock (another 1¼ cups) and cook gently for 15 minutes. The stock should just be absorbed. However small quantities of rice can dry out: watch it, and give it another couple of spoons from the chicken pot if necessary. When the rice is done, cover with another pan and leave to stand off the heat for 5 minutes. Turn off the chicken too. Serve the two dishes together, sprinkling a little chopped green onion top over the chicken. *(Serves 4)*

CUAJADA, MEL I MATO O YOGUR CON MIEL

Junket or cream cheese with honey or yoghurt

Look out for soft, fresh cream cheese and serve this with honey, called *mel i mató* in Catalonia. In the Basque country and Navarre *cuajada* is on sale in small, brown, straight-sided terracotta jars – nicer than plastic pots. This is junket or curds, a type of solidified milk, which was popular everywhere until yoghurt became so fashionable. Or try plain yoghurt (*yogur*), with *miel*, one of Spain's many flower honeys.

Fried cheese with tomato salad
Jellied red mullet and avocado
Muscatel ice cream with dessert wine

A supper for a hot night! The jellied fish are prepared in advance. The starter is hot and served with a salad. The meal ends with a liquorous ice cream.

QUESO FRITO CON TOMATE

Fried cheese with tomato salad

This familiar tapa is mainly served with bread, but tomato salad goes well with it at the beginning of a meal. Spanish onions are mellower than our white onions and can be eaten raw. Four sliced tomatoes need four onion slices, pushed into rings. Dress with pepper, salt and oil.

about 200g (7oz) medium-hard cheese	*doscientos gramos de queso, estilo Manchego*
2 tablespoons flour	*harina*
1 egg	*huevos*
breadcrumbs	*pan rallado*
6–8 tablespoons olive oil	*aceite de oliva*

Cut four neat slices of cheese, about 25g (1oz each), just under 1cm (½in) thick. Cut them across diagonally to make eight. Flour the slices, shaking off the excess. Turn them in beaten egg then dredge with breadcrumbs.

Heat the oil in a wide pan and put in the slices. Fry for a minute on each side, turning with a fish slice. They should be melted inside, without oozing. Serve at once with tomato salad. *(Serves 4)*

SALMONETES EN ESCABECHE CON AGUACATE

Jellied red mullet salad and avocado

Red mullet are easy to cook like this, and don't even need cleaning. They can be served whole to adults, or the fillets can be removed while they are hot, then cooled and served in their own jelly.

4 red mullet about 200g (7oz) each	*cuatro salmonetes, aproxidamente doscientos gramos la cada*
2 tablespoons olive oil	*aceite de oliva*
1 small onion, finely chopped	*cebolla*
1 large garlic clove, finely chopped	*ajo*
200ml (7fl oz) dry white wine	*vino blanco*
200ml (7fl oz) wine vinegar	*vinagre*
1 bay leaf or 2 sprigs thyme	*laurel o tomillo*
4 avocados	*cuatro aguacates*
salt, pepper	*sal, pimienta*
2 tablespoons sherry vinegar or wine vinegar	*vinagre de Jerez o de vino*

Remove the scales from the fish by scraping from the tail towards the head; the scales come off easily. Cut off the fins with scissors.

Heat the oil in a pan that will just hold all the fish and fry the onion gently until soft, then add the garlic. Put in the fish and pour in the wine and vinegar, adding extra if necessary to cover them, and tuck in the thyme or bay leaf. Bring to the boil, then cover, turn down the heat and simmer for 10 minutes.

Using a fish slice, move the fish carefully to a dish. The idea is to cover them with liquid, so the dish should be small and deep enough to hold four fish, or shallow and wide to hold eight fillets. Strain the cooking juices over them and refrigerate until needed. If the jelly covers them they are safe for a couple of days.

To serve, peel the avocados, cut in half and slice the flesh off the stones. Sprinkle with vinegar and seasoning and turn gently. Arrange the fish on four plates with the chopped jelly and avocado slices. Serve with bread. A chilled *rosado* wine matches the colour of the fish. *(Serves 4)*

HELADO DE PASAS DE MALAGA

Muscatel ice cream with dessert wine

The dried muscatel grapes, pasas de Malaga, are some of the finest raisins grown. Over the top pour one of Andalucia's spectacular dessert wines. The choice is wide. Viña 25 is a sherry sweetened with extra juice from Pedro Ximénez grapes, made by Domecq. You can also find Pedro Ximénez itself in some take-your-own-bottle cellars in the south, although it is becoming rarer. Lágrima is celebrated, and the cheaper Malaga dulce is also worth looking for. Oloroso sherry will do the job splendidly too.

100g (4oz) raisins	*pasas de uvas*
vanilla ice cream	*helado de vainilla*
250ml (8fl oz) dessert wine	*vino dulce*

Pour boiling water over the raisins. Leave to soak for 2 hours. Drain and fold into vanilla ice cream, then spoon this into four bowls. Pour the wine over the top. *(Serves 4)*

Deep-fried artichoke puffs with tomato sauce
Chicken with olives, hot or cold
Fresh figs

A hot starter, which goes well with a glass of wine before dinner, is followed by chicken, which can be prepared ahead and eaten cold, though children like it hot with rice.

Figs are country fare in Spain, not highly regarded because they are so common wild. To eat them, make a cross at the end opposite the stalk, then peel back the skin to reveal the juicy, seedy inside.

BUNUELOS DE ALCACHOFAS CON SALSA DE TOMATE

Deep-fried artichoke puffs with tomato sauce

Artichoke bases and hearts can be bought from supermarket freezers, and canned ones are easy to find too. Baking powder can be bought in little packets (un sobre) – literally an envelope – but don't get it mixed up with dried yeast, the same word. You can use a whisked egg white instead if you haven't any baking powder.

Making an onion sofrito is a basic part of Spanish cooking: first the onion is softened, then garlic and often parsley are added. Tomato often goes in too. This is then used for a range of dishes like sauce, rice or soup. But if you haven't time for all this, serve the puffs with lemon wedges.

HOT TOMATO SAUCE (*SOFRITO*)

1 Spanish onion, chopped	*cebolla*
2 tablespoons olive oil	*aceite de olive*
1 garlic clove, finely chopped	*ajo*
2–3 big ripe tomatoes	*tomates maduros*
parsley (optional)	*perejil*
1 teaspoon grated lemon zest	*limón*

147

ARTICHOKE PUFFS

5 tablespoons flour	*harina*
1 teaspoon baking powder	*un sobre de levadura*
salt, black pepper	*sal, pimienta*
150ml (5fl oz) beer	*cerveza*
olive oil for deep frying	*aceite de oliva*
400g (14oz) artichoke bases, defrosted if frozen	*cuatrocientos gramos de fondas de alcachofas*

Start the tomato sauce first. Heat the oil in a saucepan and cook the onion slowly, adding the garlic when it is done. Skin the tomatoes and remove the seeds. Chop the flesh and add with the sieved juice to the pan. Add 2 tablespoons chopped parsley if you have it. Leave to simmer very slowly. To finish the sauce, just before serving, check the seasonings, and stir in the lemon zest.

To cook the artichokes, put the flour and baking powder in a bowl and gradually stir in the beer.

Meanwhile heat 2.5cm (1in) of oil until a tiny piece of bread will brown in under a minute. Halve the artichoke bases and dip in batter. Fry them in 2–3 batches, separating them and turning them over in the oil with a slotted spoon. They will swell and bob to the surface and are ready when a nice brown. Drain on kitchen paper and serve immediately with the tomato sauce in a jug. *(Serves 4)*

GALLO DE CAMPO CON ACEITUNAS

Farmyard chicken with olives, *hot or cold*

*An easy southern dish, needing good ingredients but little
care. It can be eaten hot, with rice, but is better still cold.
Cutting up the chicken first reduces the amount of liquid
needed for cooking, and therefore improves the sauce or jelly.*

2 tablespoons olive oil	*aceite de oliva*
2 onions, chopped	*cebollas*
3 garlic cloves, chopped	*ajo*
salt, pepper	*sal, pimienta*
1¼kg (2lb 12oz) chicken, quartered, with backbone separated	*un pollo de un kilo y cuarto, en cuartos*
24 green olives	*aceitunas*
2 bay leaves	*hoja de laurel*
175ml (6fl oz) pale dry Montilla or sherry	*fino*

Heat the oil in a casserole. Fry the onions until soft, then add
the garlic. Salt and pepper the chicken portions and pack
these neatly into the casserole with the chicken backbone (this
is discarded later). Push the olives into the spaces. Add the
wine and bay leaves, and pour in water to almost cover the
meat. (With a bit of luck, only about 400ml (14fl oz) will be
needed.) Simmer for 30–35 minutes, then discard the
backbone. The chicken and olives can then be served hot, on
a bed of rice, well moistened with the juices.

To serve cold, spoon the chicken from the casserole, cool
for 10 minutes, then remove the bones and skin. Split the
flesh into large pieces, arrange them in a shallow dish or
mould and distribute the olives. Return the bones to the
liquid and boil for a further 10 minutes to strengthen the jelly
and increase flavour. Strain the juices into a bowl and skim off
all fat. Then pour over the chicken to cover the meat. Chill to
set. Serve with green salad. *(Serves 4)*

Raw ham with melon
Spanish seafood rice *(paella)*
Iced grapes

A menu good enough to show off at home how well you ate in Spain. *Paella* always takes time, so the starter and pudding take only a couple of minutes each.

SERRANO CON MELON

Raw ham with melon

Raw ham *(serrano)* hand-carved lengthways from the bone is always wonderful, though the best is from a ham with a black trotter (un pata negra). Ask for *cuatro tajadas ligeras de serrano*, the slices will probably be around 25g (1oz) each. Melons partner them superbly – in April there are Ogen melons, then Cantaloupes. In mid-June *el melón reticulado*, with a netted pattern, followed by the familiar honeydew; late summer brings the dark green Piel de Sapo from Lérida.

PAELLA DE MARISCOS

Spanish seafood rice

The rice is the star in paella, so it is important that the stock tastes good before you start. (Ask for the fish heads and bones for the stock: Déme los cabezas y huesos, per favor). You can do this with half wine, half water and a cube. But I find the half hour or so for fish stock is about the time needed to chop up vegetables and lay the table. And there is no extra shopping.

Spanish white wines in the French style don't have much character when cooked – except the expensive ones. It is therefore better to use vermouth or a lesser quantity of sherry with water. See page 118 for the best fish to buy.

FISH STOCK

1kg (2lb) heads and bones from the fish	*cabezas y huesos de pescados*
heads and shells from the prawns	
1 onion, chopped	*cebolla*
parsley stalks, if available	*perejil*
8 black peppercorns	*pimienta*
250ml (8fl oz) dry vermouth	*vermú seco*

PAELLA

250g (8oz) prawns	*un cuarto de gambas*
250g (8oz) small squid	*un cuarto de sepias*
250g (8oz) mussels	*un cuarto de mejillones*
4–5 tablespoons olive oil	*aceite de oliva*
1 onion, peeled and chopped	*cebolla*
½ red pepper, chopped	*pimiento rojo*
2 garlic cloves, finely chopped	*ajo*
500g (1lb) white fish	*un medio kilo de filetes de pescado*
salt, black pepper	*sal, pimienta*
paprika	*pimentón dulce*
25 saffron strands or 2g sachet saffron powder	*azafrán*
200ml (7fl oz) dry vermouth	*vermú seco*
400g (12oz) medium-grain rice	*arroz*
100g (4oz) frozen peas	*cien gramos de guisantes congelados*
chopped parsley (optional)	*perejil*

To make fish stock, simmer all the ingredients together in water to cover for 30–40 minutes, then strain. Put 700ml (24fl oz) of the resulting stock into a saucepan ready for cooking the rice.

To make the *paella*, first prepare the shellfish. To clean squid, use the tentacles to pull out everything inside, then cut off the heads above the eyes and discard everything below.

Flex the body to pop out the transparent 'spine', then wash well, rubbing off the skin. Cut into rings. To clean mussels, see page 158. Keep a few prawns unpeeled for the garnish.

Heat the oil in a 30cm (12in) *paella* pan and fry the onion and chopped pepper gently until soft, adding the garlic at the end. Cut the fish into pieces and season with salt, pepper and paprika and fry gently on both sides, on the other side of the pan. Heat the stock, pouring a little over the saffron in a cup. Put the mussels in the hot stock, cover and cook for a minute until they open. Then remove and discard the top shells.

Wash the rice (2 cups) in a sieve and drain. When the onion is soft, stir the rice into it, sprinkling with paprika. Rearrange the fish round the pan and add the stock and the saffron liquid. Distribute the squid pieces, peeled prawns, peas and mussels round the pan and bring back to the boil. Start timing now – for 20–25 minutes. If you have a heat-diffuser plate, put it under the pan. If not, a large pan on a small burner will need moving regularly.

After 10 minutes, stir the rice cautiously, then lay the unshelled prawns on top. Cook until the rice is tender to the bite. Then turn off the heat and wrap the *paella* pan in foil (*hojuela de aluminio*) to keep in the steam. Put it in a low oven for 10 minutes to absorb the last liquid. Sprinkle with parsley and serve. Traditionally red wine goes with *paella* – a Rioja *reserva*. (*Serves 4–6*)

UVAS FRESCAS

Iced grapes

An easy way to make a really chilly dessert: simply put a bunch of grapes in freezer for an hour. Or strip an equal quantity of white and black grapes from their stalks into a metal tray, then chill. Serve in bowls – refreshingly cold without having lost their flavour.

Mixed vegetable and fish salad
Sherry-roast pork with olive and nut rice
Strawberries with orange juice or oloroso

Ensalada mixta is a good salad to put together, from whatever salad or little cans are to hand, while a roast is in the oven. The meal ends with strawberries – simple but perfect – and plentiful by Easter. In Spain they are not eaten with cream, which was uncommon until universal refrigeration. Fruit juice is sprinkled over them, to bring out their flavour (try fresh orange juice), while a mature *oloroso* sherry is much used in the south.

ENSALADA MIXTA

Mixed vegetable and fish salad

In a restaurant *ensalada mixta* is not just a combination of salad vegetables but a colourful pattern which probably includes fish or *chorizo* too. To lettuce, tomatoes and onion, (*lechuga, tomates y cebolla*), add a couple of hard-boiled eggs (*huevos*) and a small can of tuna (*una lata pequeña de atún*).

You can also experiment with other little cans of fish. Try *chipirones en su tinta*, minute squid canned in their own reddish ink: there will only be one or two each. Sliced cucumber (*pepino*) can go in too. Try a dressing of olive oil and salt, and scatter with fat capers (*alcaparras*) instead of adding vinegar to make a vinaigrette.

LOMO DE CERDO ASADO CON ARROZ

Sherry-roast pork with with olive and nut rice

Roast pork loin is both easy to cook and to shop for. The accompanying rice is flavoured with chopped olives and toasted nuts or dates.

600g (1lb 4oz) boned pork loin	*seiscientos grammos de lomo de cerdo, sin huesos*
½ teaspoon salt	*sal*
1 teaspoon paprika	*pimentón dulce*
black pepper	*pimienta*
4 tablespoons olive oil	*aceite de oliva*
3 garlic cloves, squashed	*ajo*
125ml (4fl oz) medium-dry sherry or Montilla	*amontillado*

OLIVE AND NUT RICE

1 Spanish onion, chopped	*cebolla*
2 tablespoons olive oil	*aceite de oliva*
1 garlic clove, finely chopped	*ajo*
200g (7oz) medium-grain rice	*arroz*
450 ml (16fl oz) stock, made with a cube	*cubos de caldo*
a handful of green olives	*aceitunas*
12 fresh dates, chopped (optional)	*dátiles*
24 toasted almonds	*almendras*

Heat the oven to high if it is butane gas (200 C, 400 F, gas 6 if there is a regulator). Sprinkle the pork with salt, paprika and pepper and put into an oven dish into which it fits without leaving too much space. Pour in the oil, then turn the pork in this, spooning it over the ends. Add the whole, squashed garlic cloves. Roast for 1 hour 10 minutes, basting after 15 minutes.

For the rice, fry the onion in the oil in a small *paella* pan, adding the garlic when it is soft. Rinse the rice (1 cup) in a colander, drain, add to the onion and garlic in the pan and stir. Add half the hot stock. When this has been absorbed, stir and add the remaining stock and the pitted, chopped olives and dates (if using). Simmer over a very low heat for 15 minutes.

Next, pour the *amontillado* over the meat, and baste again. Toast the almonds in a dish or tray in the oven, shaking at least once.

When the rice is done, turn off the heat. Cover it with a tray or lid and let it steam for 5 minutes. Meanwhile, carve the pork into thin slices. Scatter toasted, roughly chopped nuts over the rice and lay the pork slices on top. Spoon the juices and garlic on top. *(Serves 4)*

Spicy tomato potatoes
Mussel soup
Cheese and apples

A filling potato dish is followed by one of the best mussel soups. Cheese and apples end an easy meal.

PATATAS BRAVAS

Potatoes in spicy tomato sauce

A typical way of cooking potatoes is to fry them until they have a crisp outside, then dunk them in sauce until they have absorbed it, and are moist again. The idea in the name is that these potatoes 'hold their own' – in Barcelona they can be very piquant. Brava can also mean uncivilized, and this is what happens if you make them too hot! If you buy Worcestershire sauce on holiday, this can be used, to taste, instead of chilli or cayenne. As a tapa they are served on a dish with cocktail sticks, and everyone helps themselves.

750g (1lb 8oz) potatoes, diced	*patatas*
6 tablespoons olive oil	*aceite de oliva*
SPICY TOMATO SAUCE	
2 tablespoons olive oil	*aceite de oliva*
1 Spanish onion, finely chopped	*cebolla*
2 garlic cloves, finely chopped	*ajo*
2 ripe tomatoes, skinned	*tomates maduros*
4 tablespoons white wine, or sherry	*vino blanco o fino*
½ dried hot chilli, or cayenne to taste	*guindilla o pimentón piquante*
a squeeze of lemon	*limón*

Start by making the sauce. Heat the oil in a casserole (big enough to take the potatoes as well) and cook the onion slowly. Add the garlic when the onion is soft. Meanwhile heat the oil in a *paella* pan and fry the potatoes over high heat for 5 minutes to seal them all over. Then turn down the heat and cook for another 20 minutes, stirring frequently so they do not catch.

Skin the tomatoes. Discard the seeds and chop the flesh. Add it to the casserole with the juice and wine or sherry. Season with pepper and the seeded, chopped chilli or cayenne and cook slowly until the sauce is thick. Taste, then add lemon juice, which underlines the chilli effect. Add more cayenne if required. Add the potatoes to the sauce and cook until it coats the pieces. *(Serves 4)*

SOPA DE MEJILLONES A LA CATALANA

Catalan mussel soup

Very quick to make, this is the best regional mussel soup, with a hint of anis, although a big glass of dry white wine can replace the liquor. A pleasant lunch-time variation is to stuff the shelled mussels into bocadillos (page 126) and skip the extra water and liquor entirely.

1kg (2lb) mussels	*un kilo de mejillones*
2 tablespoons olive oil	*aceite de oliva*
1 mild Spanish onion, chopped	*cebolla*
1 garlic clove, finely chopped	*ajo*
2 big ripe tomatoes	*tomates maduros*
125ml (4fl oz) *aguardiente* or *pacharán*	*aguardiente o pacharán*
salt, black pepper	*sal, pimienta*
cayenne	*cayena*
½ lemon	*limón*
chopped parsley (optional)	*perejil*
4 slices of bread	*pan*

Clean the mussels: cover them with cold water then scrub them one by one. Pull off all 'beards'. Throw out any that are smashed or do not shut when touched.

Meanwhile, heat the oil in a casserole big enough to contain everything and fry the onion gently until soft. Add the garlic. Skin the tomatoes. If the skins don't come off easily, put them into boiling water for about 10 seconds. Discard the seeds. Add the chopped tomato flesh to the casserole pan and cook until it is reduced to a sauce. Add a glass of water and bring to the boil.

Add the mussels in 2–3 batches. Cook briefly with the lid on until they open. Then use a slotted spoon to remove them to a plate and discard the top shell. Throw away any that smell really strongly, or obstinately remain shut. When they are all done, return them to the pan and sprinkle with the liquor.

Add more water – about another 500ml (18fl oz – about a pint) – and bring back to simmering. Season with salt and pepper, adding cayenne and lemon juice to taste – *pacharán* is sweet. Add chopped parsley if available. The Spanish way to serve them is to break a slice of yesterday's bread into the bottom of each bowl, then ladle the soup on top. *(Serves 4)*

CHEESE AND APPLES

One of best way to appreciate mature Spanish cheese is at the end of a meal, as Manchego-style ones are rather dry and wine sets them off well. I like the cheeses that have been stored in olive oil (*queso maduro en aceite*) Manchegos and their copies, which are strong without being totally dry. Blot well before serving. Cabrales is another stunner, the most famous blue, creamy in texture and sold all over the country.

Spanish apples make good partners. The Basque country grows an apple similar to the French Reinette and our Cox. But in Catalonia, in the foothills of the Pyrenees, *el Golden* are grown and they are fat and delicious.

Spinach Catalan style
Kidneys in sherry with pasta
Peaches in red wine or orange juice

A strongly flavoured vegetable dish is followed by popular nursery food and an easy dessert, since everybody makes their own.

Ripe peaches peel quite easily: just slice the flesh off the stone into your glass – red wine or orange juice – at the end of meal. Sprinkle with a little sugar and eat with a spoon.

ESPINACAS A LA CATALANA

Spinach with almonds and anchovies

2 tablespoons olive oil	*aceite de oliva*
3 tablespoons almonds	*almendras*
1½kg (3lb) spinach or chard	*un kilo y media de espinacas o acelgas*
½ onion, finely chopped	*cebolla*
1 garlic cloves, finely chopped	*ajo*
4 canned anchovy fillets, chopped	*una lata de anchoas*
salt, black pepper	*sal, pimienta*

Heat the oil in a pan large enough to hold at least half the leaves, and fry the almonds, turning them constantly until golden. Then put them aside and chop them.

Meanwhile wash the spinach or chard, stripping out the stalks. Drain well.

Add the onion to the oil, frying until golden. Then add the garlic. Add half the spinach or chard leaves cooking them in only the water clinging to the leaves, with the lid on. As the leaves reduce, turn the top ones to the bottom and add the remaining ones until all the leaves are soft. Break them up

159

with a spoon and drain if necessary. Stir in the chopped anchovy fillets. Season lightly, sprinkle with chopped nuts and serve. *(Serves 4)*

RINONES AL JEREZ CON FIDEOS

Kidneys in sherry with pasta

A dish served on most tapas bars in Spain. You will have noticed that a little serrano goes into most dishes in Spain. Normally it's included here too. But for a change I have used tocino (fat pork belly) or panceta – which is our streaky bacon belly, but is sold rolled up – with mushrooms. The dish can be served with long-grain rice, but this is not always easy to buy in Spain. Instead, serve it with fideos, which looks like a shorter, thinner spaghetti and cooks very fast.

1–2 tablespoons olive oil	*aceite de oliva*
100g (4oz) pork back fat, or belly, diced	*cien gramos de tocino o panceta*
1 Spanish onion, chopped	*cebolla*
1 garlic clove, finely chopped	*ajo*
8–10 lambs' kidneys	*ocho o diez riñones*
2 tablespoons flour	*harina*
250g (½lb) sliced mushrooms,	*un cuarto de champiñones*
salt, black pepper	*sal, pimienta*
100ml (3½fl oz) sherry or Montilla	*fino o amontillado*
1 tablespoon tomato paste	*concentrado de tomate*
2 sprigs thyme (optional)	*tomillo*
2 tablespoons chopped parsley (optional)	*perejil*
350g (12oz) pasta	*fideos*

Heat the oil with the diced *tocino* or *panceta* in a small *paella* pan until a little fat runs. Add the onion and fry over low heat until it is softened, stirring regularly. Then add the garlic. Meanwhile prepare the kidneys. Remove all the membrane, cutting out the middle core, and then cut into large dice. Remove the onion and ham from the pan.

Turn up the heat very high and put the kidneys into the pan in handfuls, stirring them to seal all the surfaces. Pull them to the side of the pan as you add each handful. Add a little more oil if needed. When they are all browned, return the onions and ham to the pan. Sprinkle with flour and stir in. Add the mushrooms and cook stirring until soft.

Add the sherry, tomato paste and thyme if you have it and simmer the kidneys. Season to taste, stir in the parsley and remove from the heat.

Meanwhile cook the *fideos* in large pan of boiling salted water. Time for 5 minutes or follow packet directions. Drain the pasta, stir with a tablespoon of olive oil and seasoning, and serve with the kidneys. *(Serves 4)*

Clams raw or cooked
Pork chops with paprika potatoes
Pears or caramel custards

An easy menu, because all of us can cook chops and fried potatoes without thinking – even the Spanish way – and the starter and pudding are bought.

Pears are grown in Galicia, in the north, and in Catalonia and the south as well. They have a comparatively short season. One to look for is Don Guindo. As an alternative, buy *flanes* ready-made – this caramel custard is Spain's national pudding and it is sold in foil-covered pots, like yoghurt.

ALMEJAS

Clams, raw or cooked

Small raw clams are fiddly to open, so the ideal way is to make every one do their own, as a starter.

500g (1lb) clams   *quinientos de almejas*

To open clams, poke a table knife blade between the shells. If this seems too tricky, heat 6 tablespoons *fino* in a pan with a chopped garlic clove and throw in a handful of clams. Clap on the lid and leave a minute. Then scoop these out and throw in the next lot; serve with the liquid dribbled over. Chilled *manzanilla*, most delicate of sherries, goes well with them, raw or steamed. *(Serves 4)*

CHULETAS CON PATATAS

Fried pork chops with paprika potatoes

*Paprika is the Spanish condiment, an integral part of
cooking and used before the meat goes in the pan, rather
than as a cosmetic at the end. You will need 2 good-sized
frying pans.*

PAPRIKA POTATOES

200ml (7fl oz) olive oil	*aceite de oliva*
700g (1lb 8oz) potatoes, diced	*patatas*
salt, black pepper	*sal, pimienta*
2–3 teaspoons paprika	*pimentón dulce*

4 pork chops	*cuatro chuletas de cerdo*
salt, black pepper	*sal, pimienta*
2 teaspoons paprika	*pimentón dulce*
flour	*harina*
4 tablespoons olive oil	*aceite de oliva*
1 lemon cut into 4 wedges	*limón*

The more oil used in cooking the potatoes, and the hotter it
is, the less they absorb. Heat the oil in a *paella* pan, almost
1cm (about ¼in) deep. Put in the potatoes and cook over high
heat, turning until they are sealed on all sides. Then turn
down the heat and let them cook through, stirring regularly.

Season the chops with salt, pepper and paprika, then dust
with flour, shaking off the excess. Heat the oil in a *paella* pan
and cook the chops – about 10 minutes each side, depending
on thickness. Serve with lemon squeezed over.

When the potatoes are done, use a slotted spoon to transfer
to a roasting tin lined with a double layer of kitchen paper and
shake to and fro. Drain the fat from the pan (it can be used
again). Return the potatoes to the pan, season well with salt,
pepper and paprika and heat through gently. Serve from the
pan. *(Serves 4)*

> Cooked pepper, tomato and canned tuna salad
> Individual baked eggs with green salad
> Pastries or biscuits

An easy-to-shop-for menu starts with a cooked salad of peppers and tomatoes before baked eggs and bought *pasteles* (cakes). Apple tart (*tarta de manzana*) is one of the most popular puff pastries, and I like the double pastry whirls of *palmeras de hojaldre*. Thoroughly Spanish are *mantecados* and *polvorones* – crumbly biscuits, sold wrapped in papers. The best ones contain almonds (*almendras*). These are meant to accompany a glass of something, like an *oloroso* sherry or a sweet, perfumed Spanish brandy, as they are very dry. For children, serve them with tangerines.

PIMIENTO, TOMATE Y ATÚN

Cooked pepper, tomato and canned tuna salad

Freshly cooked, this dish makes a quick hot lunch, but I like it even better cold, when the flavours have blended. You can use any of the tunas, and either in oil (en aceite), or in brine (en salmuera).

3 red peppers, seeded	*tres pimientos rojos*
4 tablespoons olive oil	*aceite de oliva*
500g (1lb) tomatoes	*un medio kilo de tomates*
1 garlic clove, finely chopped	*ajo*
175g (6oz) can of tuna	*una late de ciento setente cinco gramos de atún o bonito*
salt, black pepper	*sal, pimienta*
parsley if available	*perejil*

Cut the peppers into slim strips. Heat the oil in a *paella* pan and add the peppers. Cook, stirring occasionally, until they start to wilt and colour at the edges. Skin the tomatoes, discard seeds and juice and cut into strips. Add to the pan with the chopped garlic and cook for a further couple of minutes.

Drain the tuna and crumble it in. Season well and serve, cold or hot, scattered with flat parsley leaves, if available. Eat with crusty bread. *(Serves 4)*

CAZUELITAS DE HUEVOS AL HORNO
Individual baked eggs

The eggs are baked in individual dishes, and this recipe is quick, because it cuts out onion-frying. However if you like chicken livers – widely available in Spain – fry 250g (8oz) livers (doscientos cincuanto de higadillas), adding a couple to each dish, instead of the second egg. Fried slices of sausage, bits of ham and prawns are other possible additions, with left-over cooked vegetables.

4 teaspoons olive oil	*aceite de oliva*
350ml (12fl oz) canned tomato sauce	*una lata de tomate frito*
4 small courgettes	*calabacines*
1 large green pepper, seeded	*pimiento verde*
bunch of spring onions	*cebolletas*
2 garlic cloves, finely chopped	*ajo*
4 tablespoons parsley *(optional)*	*perejil*
4 or 8 eggs	*ocho huevos*
salt, black pepper	*sal, pimienta*
paprika	*pimentón dulce*

Heat the oven, to high if it is butane gas (200 C, 400 F, gas 6 if there is a regulator). Pour a little oil into four *cazuelitas* and smear it round the inside of the dishes. Put them into the oven to heat. Heat the tomato sauce in a saucepan.

165

Top and tail the courgettes and slice thinly. Dice the pepper and chop the spring onions, keeping the white and green parts separate.

Divide the hot tomato sauce between the dishes and sprinkle with garlic. Distribute the courgette slices and diced pepper. Sprinkle with the white of onion and the parsley (if using).

Break one or more eggs into each dish and season well with salt, pepper and paprika.

Bake for about 15 minutes, until the eggs are just set, then garnish with a little of the chopped green onion tops. Eat with bread and a green salad. *(Serves 4)*

Grey mullet baked with saffron and potatoes
Ice cream cake

Baked fish is eaten on Christmas Eve, so it has a festive feel. It is also a meal, complete in this version with vegetables. Rush an ice cream cake (*una tarta helada*) back to your apartment, in a polystyrene container, for pudding.

LISA AL HORNO CON AZAFRAN Y PATATES

Grey mullet baked with saffron and potatoes

A striped grey mullet (lisa) is often the right size for four, but red bream (besugo) and the more expensive sea bass and gilt-headed bream (lubina, dorada), are all delicious this way. To have it cleaned say: Limpiela, por favor. The picada is optional but is a traditional Spanish way of garnishing a dish. The bread and hard-boiled eggs thicken the sauce, while the bit on top of the fish crisps. You need an oval baking dish for this, at least 36cm (14in) long: check that you have one before you shop.

800g (1lb 12oz) grey mullet, cleaned	*una lisa de ochocientos gramos*
salt, black pepper	*sal, pimienta*
1½ lemons	*dos limones*
2–3 tablespoons olive oil	*aceite de oliva*
1 Spanish onion, chopped	*cebolla*
1 garlic clove, finely chopped	*ajo*
2 large tomatoes, skinned	*tomates*
4 tablespoons chopped parsley	*perejil*
200ml (7fl oz) white Rioja or dry vermouth	*Rioja blanco o vermú seco*
200ml (7fl oz) fish stock, made with a cube if necessary	*cubos de caldo de pescado*
2g saffron powder	*dos sobres de azafrán*
350g (12oz) potatoes, diced	*patates*
1 bay leaf	*hoja de laurel*

PICADA

4 tablespoons breadcrumbs	*pan*
1 tablespoon olive oil	*aceite de oliva*
2 garlic cloves, finely chopped	*ajo*
2 tablespoons chopped parsley	*perejil*
1–2 hard-boiled eggs, chopped	*huevos*

Cut off the fish fins with scissors and stroke from the tail to head to remove all the scales. Wash under running water, outside and inside, especially if you are using mullet. Slash the fish flesh across in three places each side, down to the backbone. Season these slits, and the belly cavity, with salt and pepper. Cut one lemon into six wedges and push into the slits, so that only the rind shows. Put the fish on a plate and squeeze the half-lemon into the belly.

Heat the oven to high if it is butane gas (200 C, 400 F, gas 6, if there is a regulator). Wipe a couple of teaspoons olive oil round the inside of the dish and put it to heat in the oven.

Heat 2 tablespoons of oil in a small *paella* pan and fry the onions slowly, adding the garlic when soft. Prepare the tomatoes, discarding the skin and seeds, and chopping the flesh. Chop the parsley – the easiest way to do this is to put the parsley in a mug and snip it with the tips of a pair of scissors.

Put the fish in the dish and distribute onion on both sides. Top this with chopped tomatoes and their juice, seasoning them well. Put the fish in the oven for 10 minutes.

Heat the wine and stock in a saucepan, adding a little hot stock to the saffron in a cup. Dice the potatoes, then add them to the stock and start cooking them.

Open the oven again and spoon the potatoes round the fish. Sprinkle with the parsley. Pour the hot stock and saffron stock round the fish and add the bay leaf. Return to the oven for 25 minutes, or until the potatoes are done.

To make the *picada*, grate the bread then put the crumbs into 1 tablespoon hot oil (I use the onion pan again). Turn them until they are oily. Take the pan off the heat. Mix in the chopped garlic, parsley and chopped hard-boiled eggs. Season lightly. Ten minutes before the fish is ready, scatter this over the top.

To serve, take 2 portions from the top fillet, then turn the fish over. To eat, mash the potatoes into the juices, then mop up with bread. Old-fashioned Spanish plates often have a lip, for dishes with plenty of sauce, like this one. Any juice left-over makes splendid stock. *(Serves 4)*

Mushrooms with garlic and parsley
Moorish aubergine casserole
Custard apples or seasonal fruit

A menu for vegetarians, with all the charm of seasonal vegetables. Both the cooked courses are eaten with bread. *Rebanada*, the word for a slice of bread also means a 'wipe round the plate'. You'll quickly discover that Spain is a very mountainous country and Spaniards like nothing better than mushroom expeditions. In September the pickers crowd the roadside, selling *setas*, the general term for wild mushrooms.

Custard apples (*anonas*), are a late summer fruit, cut in half, then eaten with a spoon, they have the creaminess of real custard. Just spit out the black seeds.

CHAMPIGNONES AL AJILLO

Mushrooms with garlic and parsley

This dish is usually made with wild mushrooms, but here I have used champiñones (button mushrooms). It is cooked the same way – but locals would eat a quarter-kilo each!

500g (1lb) mushrooms	*un medio de champiñones*
2–3 tablespoon olive oil	*aceite de oliva*
2 small garlic cloves, chopped	*ajo*
salt, black pepper	*sal, pimienta*
2 tablespoon finely chopped parsley	*perejil*

Mushrooms in Spain are thoroughly dirty, so cut the ends of the stems off and decide whether to peel or wipe the caps, then slice them. Heat the oil in a *paella* pan and add the chopped garlic and sliced mushrooms. Cook gently for 5 minutes, turning them over occasionally with a wooden spoon. Season and sprinkle with parsley. *(Serves 4)*

ALBORONIA

Moorish aubergine casserole

*This is an old, old dish, also called boronia, which was
updated about 300 years ago, by adding tomatoes and
peppers. In Mallorca it contains potatoes too, and is called
tumbet – something to do with laying down slices. Other
possible additions are herbs – use plenty of basil if you have
it – or fruit, gypsy-style, using an apple or a pear.
The whole thing can be cooked on top of the stove, stirring it
as it cooks, but I find it easier to wait a little longer and let
it cook unwatched in the oven. It is excellent reheated or
cold, and is a nice partner to bread and salami-style
sausages.*

1 large aubergine	*berenjena*
salt, pepper	*sal, pimienta*
6 tablespoons olive oil	*aceite de oliva*
1 large Spanish onion	*cebolla*
2 garlic cloves, finely chopped	*ajo*
4 small courgettes	*calabacines*
2 big green peppers, seeded	*dos pimientos verdes*
3 x 400g (14oz) cans tomatoes	*tres latas de tomates de cuatro cientos gramos*
1 teaspoon paprika	*pimentón dulce*
2 tablespoon vinegar	*vinagre*

Slice the aubergine very thinly, lay out on the draining board
and sprinkle with salt. Leave to sweat for at least 30 minutes.
Heat the oil in a pan and fry the onion over low heat until
soft, then add the garlic. Heat the oven to high if butane gas
(200 C, 400 F, gas 6 if there is a regulator). Wipe oil round
the inside of an earthenware *cazuela* and heat this too. Slice
the courgettes thinly and dice the peppers.

When the aubergine has exuded plenty of juice, rinse in a
couple of batches in a colander under running water and blot

with kitchen paper (*papel de cocina*).

Make three layers in the casserole, starting with a third of the aubergine slices, then scattering courgette, pepper and onion. Add two-thirds of the first can of tomatoes with the juice, smashing them up well. Season with paprika and repeat. Sprinkle vinegar over the second layer and make sure all the oil from the frying pan goes into the dish. Cover with wide foil, (*hojuela aluminio*), and put in the oven for 1½ hours. Serve with bread. Good hot or cold. *(Serves 4)*

Chickpea salad
Barbecued tuna with grilled spring onions
Savoury orange salad
Barbecue baked vegetables

My experience of barbecues is that there is a lot of hanging about. The barbecue makers lark around and don't get the fire going soon enough, and lunch is at least an hour later than usual. A substantial first course fills the gap.

The fish, when it comes, is then quite filling, best eaten with a salad. It is a pity to waste the heat, so vegetables go on the grid too, and are ready after the fish is finished. The meal fills a family for the best part of a day, and needs no pudding.

ENSALADA DE GARBANZOS

Chickpea salad

Chickpeas play the same role in Spain as potatoes do in Britain. They are very pleasantly nutty. Dried ones double their weight when soaked overnight in plenty of cold water, or for an hour in boiling water. Supermarkets also sell them ready-soaked: garbanzos en remojo. Soaked chickpeas need a minimum of an hour cooking, sometimes twice this. However, boiling them requires absolutely no effort. Adding chopped raw vegetables to the cooked chickpeas makes an easy salad. I use a few spoonfuls of ready-canned tomato sauce, with oil, for the dressing. Depending on what is to follow, half a can of chopped anchovy fillets, or chopped salchichón, the Spanish salami, make other good additions.

If you buy double the weight given in the recipe, you can add tomato sauce and fried sausages to the remainder for another quick and simple dish later.

250g (8oz) dried chickpeas, soaked	*garbanzos*
or 500g (1lb) soaked chickpeas	*un medio de garbanzo en remojo*
2 large tomatoes, skinned	*tomates*
1 red pepper, seeded	*pimiento rojo*
1 green pepper, seeded	*pimiento verde*
2–3 tablespoons chopped Spanish onion	*cebolla*
6 tablespoons tomato sauce	*tomate frito en lata*
2 tablespoons olive oil	*aceite de oliva*
salt, black pepper	*sal, pimienta*
cayenne	*pimentón piquante*
parsley	*perejil*

Cover the soaked chickpeas generously with water. Bring them to the boil, then leave to simmer, covered. Try one after an hour and give them another 30 minutes if they seem too crisp. When they are done, drain in a colander.

Remove the seeds from the tomates and discard the juice. Chop the flesh. Dice the peppers and onion to the same size.

Stir the tomato sauce and oil into the chickpeas and season generously, adding a little cayenne. Add all the vegetables with a good 6 tablespoons parsley, if it is available. *(Serves 4)*

BONITO O ATÚN A LA BARBACOA CON CEBOLLONES

Barbecued tuna with grilled spring onions

Steaks cut from across the tail of a small bonito are best, they have the lightest white-fleshed meat. You can recognize a bonito by its scaleless, submarine-shaped body and the black bars radiating towards the tail. Atún, the blue-finned tuna has much denser meat, dark like meat steaks, and you will find that 100g (4oz) per person is usually enough.

Marinading ahead is particularly important for this dense fish. Put it in marinade the moment you get back from shopping. Grill the steak whole and partition it afterwards. The expensive swordfish (pez espada) is cooked in the same way, and this marinade will serve for all other fish and chicken.

600g (1lb 4oz) tuna steak	*seisceintos gramos de bonito o atún*

MARINADE

½ onion, chopped	*cebolla*
4 garlic cloves, finely chopped	*ajo*
salt, black pepper	*sal, pimienta*
2 teaspoons coriander seeds (optional)	*culantro*
1 bay leaf	*hoja de laurel*
6 tablespoons olive oil	*aceite de oliva*
1 teaspoon grated lemon peel	*limón*
juice of 2 lemons	

Combine the marinade ingredients, crushing the chopped garlic into the salt with the flat of a knife. Crush the coriander seeds between two spoons. Rub this mixture into the fish steak in a shallow dish, and leave as long as possible, preferably out of the fridge. Turn occasionally, or spoon the oil back over it.

When the barbecue charcoal has died down to a cooking heat, grill the steak for 10 minutes on each side, depending on thickness. Brush it with the remnant of the marinade, or more oil, as you turn it. Grill spring onions at the same time (see below), and serve with orange salad and bread. *(Serves 4)*

ENSALADA DE NARANJA

Savoury orange salad

It's worth remembering that oranges make a very good salad to accompany fish. You can eat this as another starter, if the barbecue is very slow in getting going.

4–6 oranges	*cuatro o seis naranjas*
5 tablespoons *fino* sherry or *montilla*	
3 tablespoons olive oil	*aceite de oliva*
salt and pepper to taste	*sal, pimienta*
a few olives, chopped onion, or spring onion tops (all optional)	*aceitunas, cebolla, cebolletas*

Peel the oranges, removing the outside membrane and slice them. Dress them in a bowl with the *fino* sherry or Montilla and the olive oil. Season with salt and pepper. Scatter with olives or a tablespoonful of chopped onion, or green spring onion tops, if you like. *(Serves 4)*

ESCALIVADA

Barbecue baked vegetables

This Catalan word covers anything baked on the cinders – a fairly lengthy process for most vegetables. The only vegetable that cooks as fast as fish are spring onions (*ceballones*). Buy them as fat as you can, and trim the tops. Brush everything that goes on the grill generously with oil. It doesn't matter if the outside chars.

Tomatoes (*tomates*) but are well worth baking round the fish – to eat with pepper and salt after the fish is finished.

If you like aubergine purée (*berenjenas*), then grill small ones, turning them regularly, to use later.

CHAPTER NINE

CHILDREN AND BABIES

It's very enjoyable to travel with a child to a country like Spain where everyone adores children so much. It's also a good way of meeting people. If you are with a child, people will immediately take an interest in you, and out will come the photos of their own families. You will learn some Spanish and perhaps make a contact who may help you.

You can also take children with you anywhere – and at any time. Children sleep for a long time in the heat of the afternoon, and it is common to see a family on the evening *paseo* (walkabout) with the baby too. There are very few taboos – perhaps only in the smartest restaurants – on admitting children. In restaurants they are allowed to behave like children in adult parties too, getting down from the table between courses and talking naturally. As a consequence of this liberty, many Spanish children acquire social manners very early and don't seem to be noisy or obstreperously try to attract attention when among adults.

CHILDREN'S FOOD *(alimentos para niños)*

The Spanish child's day starts with a big cup of hot chocolate for breakfast. This is an excellent way to drink local milk which is homogenized, and not particularly nice alone. The chocolate powder for this is sold ready-mixed with a thickener, and makes a drink thick enough to dip bread into. Nesquik chocolate also makes a good cold drink.

Since the cooked meals are widely spaced children also get *una merienda*, an afternoon snack of bread (often with cheese) or perhaps a cake, which is equivalent to our tea-time. Otherwise, children eat what adults eat, although the husband may sometimes be given meat and the children only the vegetables.

It is easy to find look-alikes for food that children enjoy at home. Freezers usually contain breaded fish – the Spanish invented fish fingers. However Spanish food has more taste than the very bland foods that children become accustomed to in British schools. These fingers definitely taste of cod. Canned cooked beans are widely sold, but are likely to be spicy or have sausage in them. Bland Dutch cheeses, like red-rinded Edam, are on sale in supermarkets, and taste less strong than local ones. Yoghurt (*yogur*) is universal, as are pots of ready-made custard puddings.

Cornflakes are available, but not necessarily everywhere. Tomato ketchup is widely sold, just called *salsa de tomate*. Try telling your children that in Spain they put the ketchup in the sausages when they make them, and introduce them to red *chorizos*.

EATING OUT *(comer en un restaurante)*

Tapas bars are a wonderfully convenient institution, for dad and mum can have a beer and the children a full meal. They sell food that children like, in particular meat balls in tomato sauce (*albóndigas*). Try also *un estofado de ternera*, a veal stew in gravy. Every restaurant menu has roast chicken and pork chops – and chips (*patatas fritas*) are a national passion. To get a side-order, ask for *una ración*. Most children like fried squid rings (*calamares*) which vaguely resemble pasta.

Since restaurant helpings are usually enormous, small children eat bits of their parents' portions. Ask for a second plate (*un otro plato*) and some spoons (*unas cucharillas*).

179

SHOPPING FOR BABIES *(las compras para bebe)*

Canned babyfood *(alimento para bebe)* is widely available in supermarkets. Your holiday kitchen is very unlikely to contain a blender or a *mouli-legumes* for preparing food freshly. However, a small blender will run off the Spanish power without any problems, so if you need one of these, take your own.

One particularly convenient feature of larger food shops (and some specialist corner shops too) are freezers with open packs. From these it is possible to buy as small a quantity of frozen food as you wish – good for child meals.

Except for things like nappies (see below) the general rule is: take your own, if it is not too big. If you need a new feeding bottle, ask for *un biberón*. New teats are *unas tetinas para un biberón*. If you want to ask for one with a smaller (or larger) hole, *¿Tiene unas tetinas con agujero mas pequeño (grande)?* I would rely on boiling water for sterilizing, but you can buy Milton. A dummy is *un chupete*.

TOILETS AND NAPPIES *(los servicios y pañales)*

Public toilets are infrequent, although bus and railway stations have them in major cities. As a result restaurants and bars everywhere are good-tempered about non-customers walking in and using theirs. However, these can be dirty. There is often no paper and you can avoid much misery by keeping a supply of tissues *(tissus)* in readiness. Hotels and big shops like Woolworths and El Corte Inglés perform a useful public function by having big toilets. Some of the larger supermarkets have cafés and bars which have them too. On most beaches there are restaurant-bars set up on the sand at regular intervals, which also have cabins out the back. You will probably have to ask for the key to these: *la llave por los servicios, por favor.*

In tiny country places, where they are not used to tourists, you may still find the two-foot squat hole, with a chain-flushing system. While they are OK once you've got the idea, they are definitely off-putting at first. People consequently show a certain tolerance to the needs of small children. But it's still a good idea to keep a potty in the car.

Nappies are *pañales*, and disposable nappies (*que se puede tirar*) are widely sold. These do NOT go down the toilet. In many places in Spain even paper does not flush away. The reason is that toilets are normally built on cesspits and there is not sufficient water to constantly dredge and dissolve paper, or for central collection and sewage. You will see a waste-paper basket provided for paper in public conveniences. Nappies also go in this, so keep a few plastic bags with your clean supply, for disposing of the soiled ones.

BEACHES (*las playas*)

Beaches can be hazardous places for small children, who often play naked at the edge of the water for a considerable time without feeling the heat. There is a great deal of reflected light and this can take its toll, especially on the south and east coasts. Unlike adults, children do not usually wear sun-glasses. A hat with a peak can reduce this problem – and sun hats are a must anyway. For protection against the sand you will need a beach mattress, grass mat, vast towel or rug. Small, wet bottoms can get sore even on fine sand, and a resting place is needed.

Getting a family of children onto a beach with everything they need for a day, through the day, then home again with tempers more or less intact and nothing forgotten, requires quite a lot of organization. I use a series of bags, which everyone recognizes, and which always have the same things packed in them. For example, a waterproof beach bag that takes beach toys and everyone's towels and costumes. Then another perhaps with mum's handbag, creams, sun specs, and some loose change for hiring umbrellas and buying drinks, books and magazines. Then another for drinks and fruit. After a day or so, things get packed correctly and panic is reduced.

Allocate one piece of equipment to each child – a rubber ring, flippers, an umbrella. By always carrying the same thing, the child comes to feel responsible for it.

Spanish families tend to make a morning of it and then go home at 2 or 3 for lunch and a nap indoors, returning later in the afternoon. Morning and late afternoon beach parties are in fact best, because in the middle of the day the sun is at its strongest and most harmful. A small baby in a pushchair is particularly at risk at this time. If you are spending the whole day on the beach, a big umbrella (*un quitasol*) gives a good depth of shade, and most beaches hire them out, usually with a couple of loungers, which make a family camp for about £1 or so a day.

Small children have delicate flesh and burn very easily. They need greasing with sun creams with a high-blocking factor. Some beaches have fresh-water showers near the exit steps (although often these don't work). It is also essential to cream up at night, to keep flesh moist, with an after-sun cream (or Nivea will do).

For bad burns see HEALTH, Chapter 11.

Spanish beaches are not well provided with life guards. It is unlikely that you will let your children swim out of sight, but lilos and rubber boats do constitute a risk. The Atlantic is tidal, and although the Mediterranean is not, some beaches on the south coast have a strong sideways drift. You can also get separated quite easily when children get into activities with neighbouring families – the umbrellas look identical. Identify your family camp by some landmark (like a shopfront or flagpole) that can be seen from the sea shore.

MOSQUITOES AND ANTS *(mosquitos y hormigos)*

Ants are attracted by babies – both by their pleasant smell and by nappies. Wet nappies will make an invisible print on the floor. You can't see it, but the ant can smell it and will be there shortly. So mop floors where babies sit and crawl regularly. Glasses with fruit juice or any sort of food will also attract ants.

A baby sleeping next to an open window in a shared room is usually the first to get bitten. Though kitchens and sometimes back windows or cupboard windows may have fly-screens over them, if you go to the bedroom to check the baby and turn on the light when the windows are open, you will bring in a host of insects. If you decide to buy a mosquito net to cover a cradle, this is *una red para mosquitos*. It is only safe for a baby that is too young to pull the net down into the cradle. You may prefer other methods: plug-in devices with a pill that gives off vapour as it dissolves in heat (*metamosquitas eléctrico*) are available in the areas most visited by tourists, as are insect-repellent candles. But it is probably better to buy a small plug-in device from Boots before you go and take it with you. Otherwise you will have to rely on insect-repellent creams and sprays (*un repele de mosquitos*) and bite-soothers (*una crema antihistamica*).

CACTUSES *(cactuses)*

Many driveways have cactus plants and there are many types. Their function is to keep people out, and they are a considerable danger to children playing hide-and-seek, particularly at night.

There are two sorts to watch out for. The rigid dry ones like *agave* have huge rosettes with great spikes on the ends of stiff leaves; these are particularly dangerous to the eyes. If a child does get spiked seek medical help at once. Sometimes the tips go into arms and legs and break off, then seem to cause no pain or trouble. Have these dealt with when you get home, with a local anasthetic, as they can cause gangrene later if left untended.

Equally common, and the more frequent cause of trouble, are the spiny succulents like prickly pears that have little bunches of spines on fleshy pads. It is quite easy to pick up a few of these, even from the ground, and feet in sandals are very vulnerable. Start by trying to pick them out, one by one, with eyebrow tweezers. If they are visible very near the surface, a needle can be used in the same way as one removes thorns. However cactus spines are softer and break off. To remove these, soak a pad with lemon juice (it stings a bit, but is not an ordeal) and bind it over the spines for a few hours. It should pull them to the surface, where they can be picked out. If this doesn't work, seek medical help, starting at a pharmacy (*un farmacía*). The same treatment works for getting spines from sea urchins (*erizos*) out of the feet.

BABYSITTERS *(una viglia a los niños)*

If you are taking a package holiday, or are going to a block of holiday apartments, ask about babysitters before you leave. Friendly neighbours are not so difficult to find, especially if you are with other English people. You can ask for *una viglia*, or *una niñera* (nanny).

The main difficulty about Spanish babysitters is that they will not be able to speak English. For a small baby, whose needs can be coped with if he or she wakes, this doesn't matter. It is far more of a problem for a small child who wakes in night and wants Mummy.

In the daytime, you may well find that other children come to call on you, if your children are of an age to play in the street. This is particularly true in a *barrio* or an *urbanización*, which often have a village feel. Spanish children have a very long summer holiday – schools shut from July 1 to September

14. During this time the younger ones generally are looked after by their older brothers and sisters. The chances are that your children will get attached to one of these groups during the time that you are in the apartment washing or cooking. Children seem to play quite happily without a common language.

Check also whether there are nursery services provided, and whether there is an organized beach camp, where children can enroll for a couple of hours each morning for communal exercise or activity.

CHAPTER TEN

PRACTICAL HOUSEKEEPING

This chapter tells you about the vital basics of your holiday apartment – electricity, gas, rubbish, plumbing, etc. You will find other practical domestic information in WELCOME TO SPAIN (Chapter 5).

ELECTRICITY

Local electricity in Spain is an alternating 220/225 volts in most areas now, but the 125 volt supply is still used in places. If it's 220/225 volts a small blender, hairdryer or radio from Britain will work without problems, with a round two-pin plug, or a continental adaptor. The word for a plug and a socket is the same – *el enchufe*. Plugs are wired to the international standard (brown for live, blue for neutral, green-and-yellow for earth). The word for a battery is *báteria* or *pila*. Electric light bulbs are *bombillas*.

Spanish plugs are not fused and older properties often have the whole apartment running on one or two fuses. Find out where the fuse box (*la caja de plomos*) is early on. It's probably behind the front door, or in a kitchen cupboard. Spare fuses cannot be bought ready-charged. Fuses which blow have to be removed, a new wire (*hilo para plomos*) inserted and screwed in, and then the fuse replaced. A screwdriver is *un destornillador*. If the fuse box is not in the apartment, and there is a caretaker to the apartment block, tell him that the light has fused: *Se ha fundido el plomo*.

BUTANE GAS OVEN *(un horno butano)*

Butane gas cylinders are easy to use. Press down the brass cap
onto the nozzle of a new cylinder (there's a diagram on it).
When it's secure, the cap just flicks across. Check that you
have a spare full one (it's usually stored under the sink) when
the one you're using begins to feel light. Ask where the refills
can be obtained: *¿Dónde puede conseguir gas butano?* Take the
empty blue or orange cylinder back to the shop when you
collect a new one.

Gas needs permanent ventilation, and an open window
when you are cooking; it's also best to shut the cap off when
you go out. The usual courtesy is to leave a full cylinder for
the next occupants – this will cost you less than a fiver.

LAVATORY *(el servicio)*

Rule one is not to put down the lavatory anything that doesn't
absolutely have to go there. In most of Spain water is a
comparatively scarce commodity and the systems aren't built
with massive gushes to sweep everything away. Country
places either have cesspits, or the waste runs into the local
streams – domestic water is recycled for agriculture. Cesspits
are very efficient, not smelly, and a great deal better than
public drains that dry out for lack of water.

If the cistern isn't filling, it may be because there's a water
stoppage. Check to see whether your taps are running. These
stoppages are random in dry weather, but rarely last longer
than five hours. If your area is prone to stoppages, keep some
water on hand; a bucketful down the toilet will clear it
temporarily. A bucket is *un cubo.*

For other failures, call the plumber *(el fontenero)*. Tell him
that the lavatory isn't working: *El water no functiona.*

RUBBISH *(las basuras)*

The rubbish service in Spain is really excellent, with daily removal, except on holidays and saints' days. Check whether you have bins on your apartment level, or have to take the bags down to the public bin *(el cubo de basuras)*.

Rubbish is tied into the usual black bags *(bolsas de basuras)*. It's a familiar evening sight in villages to see all the *basuras* bins coming out, with their lids tightly closed against cats and dogs, who have rather a poor diet in regions where the population is also poor.

You will also pass gulleys *(arroyos)* with evil-smelling town rubbish, which are also evilly sited, and see a great deal of litter scattered round the countryside, or just dumped in bags by the roadside. At the death of Franco in 1975, living standards in Spain were lower than in Ireland, and there has been a marked depopulation of the countryside. The struggle to industrialize has gone well, but this is not a process that encourages conservation of the countryside and 'green' living.

ANTS AND MOSQUITOES *(hormigos y mosquitos)*

Ants are attracted to people, and usually it's a lack of experience with them that brings them inside and not the fault of the property itself. Ants can sense a dirty sock or an unwashed glass under a bed. They will find the uneaten peach in the paper bag in the bedroom, or the apple core left on a windowsill. A rubbish bin not completely closed by a lid attracts a marching army! And don't leave the washing-up overnight, or food in a dish in the oven – you'll regret it. Keep food in the fridge, or in plastic bags hanging up – although ants may find these eventually. Casseroles with the lid on can also be used for fruit if the fridge is full.

Distinguish between different types of rubbish up to the moment of carrying out the black bags. A waste-paper basket can take paper and anything that is not of ant-interest. Food should go into a bag-lined bucket with a tight lid.

Pressurized containers of spray (*un atomizador para hormigos*) will cause instant ant-death, so one is handy for the kitchen. After cleaning up, scatter brown ant powder (*polvo para hormigos*) onto any path that they have used. This is also effective for window-sills and other places where they file in.

Keeping out mosquitoes requires a routine. The chief thing is not to open windows when the lights are on. There is normally mosquito netting over kitchen windows. It's a good routine to shut windows and blinds when you go out in the morning, before the day's heat gets up. (See also CHILDREN AND BABIES, Chapter 9.)

LAUNDRY (el lavadero)

There are no laundrettes (*una lavandería automatica*), although occasionally they are built for tourist blocks, and you will be lucky to get a washing machine. However most Spanish apartments have a balcony or patio, and washing dries easily in a couple of hours.

You may be able to send clothes away to a laundry (*una lavandería*). Ask how soon they will be ready: *¿Cuándo estará lista?* You may also want clothes pressed if you have no iron: *¿Quiero que planchen esta ropa?*

Dry cleaning (*limpieza en seco*) outside a major town may be slow. Some villages can only manage an eight-day, send-away service. Ask: *¿Cuándo estará lista?* (When will they be ready?)

BLOCKED DRAIN (desagüe atascado)

Sand from the feet is a common cause of blocked bidet and bath drains, so try to wash your feet, or dust them well, before you come home and bath. Bidets often have an accessible U-bend at the back. If sand is the cause, a plunger (*un chupón para desagües*) will often shift it.

Don't put any vegetable rubbish or liquid meat fat down the kitchen sink. Wipe out greasy pans with paper before washing. If the sink does get blocked, try clearing it with the *chupón* first. If that doesn't work, move everything out from underneath the sink, arm yourself with a bucket and try to remove the U-bend to clear the obstruction. If this doesn't work, let the water subside for a couple of hours. If it doesn't budge at all, the block could be caused by fat, and caustic soda (*soda para desagües*) should shift this. Replace the U-bend and bail out the sink as well as you can. Boil a large pan of water and put a few spoonfuls of caustic soda down the sink. Mix about a cupful more soda with 1 litre (2 pints) of boiling water and pour this down the sink, standing well back.

If this doesn't work, call the plumber (*el fontenero*). Tell him you have a blocked kitchen-sink (handbasin, bath): *La fregadero (jofaina, baño) está atascado(a)*.

GETTING HELP

To find help of any sort go to the Yellow Pages (*las páginas amarillas*). Spanish telephone books are helpfully arranged village by village, and not alphabetically within a given region. Like this it is easy to check if there is a plumber (*fontenero*) or electrician (*electricista*) in your village or the next one. And if you happen to be on the Costa Brava, where the handyman is a professional too, *un lampista* might get you out of your jam.

CHAPTER ELEVEN

WHILE YOU'RE IN SPAIN

SURVIVAL SHOPPING

This A–Z section covers essential items that can sometimes be bought from a large supermarket (*hipermercado*) and you should have no trouble finding them. But if you don't have one near you, the following list may help you locate them.

As a special note, one source of survival shopping is the pharmacy. There are plenty of pharmacies (*farmacias*) in medium-sized villages and towns, and they operate a rota system, so that one is always open, seven days a week, until about 10 p.m. There should be a list posted outside each of those that are shut, giving the addresses of others, and also a list in the local newspaper.

In Spain, as in other continental countries, pharmacies have a major prescriptive role, and so have a much more medical look to them. They are not general stores like chemists in Britain, but do stock some cosmetics. Usually all you have to do is show the injury or describe the trouble, and they will sell you something suitable. Self-service is unusual. They also sell antibiotics, which would be prescription-only in Britain.

USEFUL PHRASES AT THE PHARMACY

I have a headache and need aspirins: *Tengo dolor de cabeza; hace falta aspirinas.*

I want to buy plasters for blisters (a graze): *Quiero esparadrapos para ampollas (un arañazo).*

I need something for mosquito bites: *Quieroalgas para picaduras de mosquito.*

Have you got an anti-insect cream (spray)?: *¿Tiene una crema (pulverizador) que se puede repeler mosquitos?*

A–Z

- calamine lotion (*loción calamina*) From the chemist.
- can opener (*abrelatas*) Look for this in the hardware shop (*ferretería*), or the supermarket.
- contact lens fluid (*solucíon por lentillas*) You will find this at the optician (*óptico*) or chemist (*farmacía*). Many of the brands of solution are international, so you may find familiar bottles. *Lentillas permeable* are gas permeable.
- contraceptive pill (*píldora*, or *anticonceptivos*) From the chemist. The chemist can supply the pill (and other drugs) without prescription. If you can tell him the brand you normally use, he can refer to the international list of equivalent drugs and supply you with the right one.
- contraceptives (*preservativos* or *condones*) From the chemist, too.
- corkscrew (*sacacorchos*) From the hardware shop (*ferretería*), again, but they are very likely to be on sale elsewhere.
- nappies (*pañales*) The chemist will stock these, as will many supermarkets (where they'll be cheaper). Familiar brands of disposables are available. Nappy rash cream is *crema para culitos*.
- pan scourer (*estropajo*) From the supermarket.
- plasters (*esparadrapos*) From the chemist.
- spectacles (*gafas*) The *óptico* may be able to provide a new pair, easier if you have your prescription.
- tampons (*tampones higénicos*) and sanitary towels (*unas compresas*) From chemists, small supermarkets and grocers.
- underwear (*ropa interior*) From boutiques, mother and baby shops, or knitting shops.
- watch batteries (*pilas de reloj*) From jewellers (*joyería*) or watch and clock shops (*relojería*).

LOCAL SERVICES

BANKS

There has been a great proliferation of banks: there are banks everywhere. But in Spain any process, even money-changing, is very, very slow, and the installation of computers seems to have slowed things up even more. For changing money it is better to use the larger banks if you can – Banco Central, Banco de Bilbao, Banco de Santander or Banco Hispano-Americano. They tend to charge less commission than the smaller ones. They are also better than the exchanges (*cambios*), although these are open longer hours. Banks are less formal places than used to be – the staff often wear jeans – but a passport is still necessary for changing money: a cash card is not sufficient identification. Building societies (*casas de ahorros*) also change money.

Banks are open Monday to Friday from 9 a.m. to 2 p.m., and Saturdays 9 a.m. to 1 p.m., although in summer they may close an hour or so earlier. Saturday closing also applies on the day before a public holiday too. The 'bridges' (*los puentes*) – the Friday and Saturday between a feast day that falls on a Thursday and the following Sunday – are also taken as holidays by the banks.

TRANSPORT

If you have no car, there a number of other ways of getting around, although few of them are fast.

BUSES (*el autobús*)

Buses are good, frequent and cheap, as rural transport is crucial in areas, particularly the south and west, where not every family owns a car. This is not a fast method of transport, as they make frequent stops. In a town most passers-by will know where *el estación de autobús* (the bus station) is. In villages it will probably be the principal bar.

The bus station has an office with time tables (*horarios*) where you can buy your tickets (*billetes*). It's cheaper to buy *ida y vuelta*, there and back. Children under four travel free.

Useful Phrases

How do I get to. . .?: *¿Cómo se llega a. . .?*
What time does the bus leave?: *¿A qué hora se va el autobús?*
How long does the journey take?: *¿Cuánto dura el viaje?*
At what times are the return buses?: *¿A qué horas son las vueltas?*
Where is the bus stop?: *¿Dónde está la parada de autobus?*

TRAINS *(el tren)*

The national service is run by RENFE and the super-train, the TALGO, will speed you across the country in air-conditioned comfort, with a restaurant car, although you may pay 75% over the lowest price for the privilege. The red *Electrotrén* and the blue diesel TER are almost as fast.

For local trips you are likely to travel more slowly. If the train is named *expreso* be warned that it isn't. The *expresos* are a night service and are slow. However, they have bunk accommodation, stacked up in three tiers with a clean sheet, where you can sleep reasonably well, although there is little room for luggage. The *rápido* is also painfully slow – it is the same service by day. However it may be useful if you want to get to somewhere nearby, and it is good way of making contact with Spaniards. There are also a number of very local train services, which are more like local buses, with mainly standing room: *Trancia (Tm)*, *Omnibús (Omn)*, *Automotor (Auto)*, *Semi-directo (Semi-dir)* and *Ferrobús (Ferro)*.

There are blue days (*días azules*), discount days when tickets are 25% cheaper. Supplements are charged to travel on the TALGO, TER and *Electrotrén*. Porters' charges on stations are regulated and they carry a tariff (*la tarifa*), so you can ask to see this if you think you are being overcharged.

Children under four travel free.

TAXIS *(el taxi)*

Taxis are generally cheaper than in Britain, because fewer people own cars. Travel within a city is cheap, and outside popular cafes you will find taxi ranks that often operate a 24-hour service. Taxi ranks are marked with a 'T' and most towns have a radio service – look in the Yellow Pages (*Paginas Amarillos*).

Since they are accustomed to family hire, taxi-drivers are generally very obliging. Many taxis run on butane gas for economy, and they will pile luggage on the top of the taxi. However they may be restricted from taking more than four adults at a time. Taxi signs – *libre* and *occupado* – are easy to understand. At night they show a green light on top when free.

Many trips, for example from the airport to a specific part of town or a hotel, are regulated, and taxis must carry these price lists, and show them if asked. Give your destination, then say: *la tarifa, por favor*. However, if you then have to cross the village or *urbanización*, they may reasonably demand a supplement, as they may in the small hours of the morning. Tips of 5% are expected on top of a metre rate or a tariff bill – but not on a quote for a journey.

EXPLORING BY OTHER MEANS

Twenty years ago donkeys were common as a means of transport in the south and rural areas. Now they have been replaced, often by the *velo* (moped) with its persistent noise. *Velo* shops are common, and you can hire them quite easily – but make sure that you have proper insurance cover. It's a useful form of transport if there are only two of you.

In areas where there are a lot of tourists there will be donkey rides through the village for children, and donkey traps, often with gay sunshades. There are also organized donkey safaris (*burro safaris*) into nearby hills from many beach centres. These are often a day-trip, with a hot Spanish lunch supplied in a picnic place. While they may not be very ambitious, it is a way to get away from the beach without having to carry small children, which makes walking uphill such hard work in hot weather. Look for advertisements in shops or the local paper.

TELEPHONE *(el teléfono)*

Spain had well-designed modern telephones long before Britain, probably because a lower proportion of the population has a phone. The cost of local calls is higher than in Britain. Telephone boxes *(cabina telefónica)* take 5, 25 and 100 peseta coins. Avoid using hotel phones if you can, as they add at least 25% commission.

Telephone books list people and establishments village by village, rather than in an alphabetical list of everyone within a designated area. There is also a Yellow Pages *(las Paginas Amarillas)* for professional help. Thus if you want a local plumber *(fontanero)* doctor *(médico)*, or *taxi*, you can quickly see what's available locally.

For international calls see CONTACT WITH HOME in this Chapter.

HAIRDRESSER *(la peluqueria)*

Hairdressers are good and cheap, so you might like a shampoo and set *(un lavado y marcardo)* during your holiday. Ask: Can I make an appointment for this afternoon? *¿Puedo pedir hora para esta tarde?* A tip of 5% above the bill is appropriate.

NEWSPAPERS *(periódicos)*

If you read Spanish, or can stagger along in it, the leading paper is *El País*, which was established post-Franco, so it is liberal, and it has separate editions in Madrid and Barcelona. *ABC* is the conservative paper, while *Ya* is Catholic. There is also *El Periódico* in Barcelona and *Diario 16* in Madrid. However, Spain has no equivalent of our 'popular' press, and newspaper reading is largely a middle-class habit.

The magazine stands *(quioscos)* in Las Ramblas in Barcelona and the Gran Via in Madrid sell an enormous number of glossy magazines. *Cambio 16* is the leading news magazine, but well over half of all magazine sales are of glossies like *!Hola!* dedicated to gossip about the famous.

British papers arrive one or two days late, and cost at least twice the usual price. Weekend newspapers are sold without their colour magazines. The American *Herald Tribune* is available on the day it is printed and is reasonably widely distributed. If you're in Madrid, look out for *In Spain*, a glossy monthly, or the fortnightly *Madrid Visitor*. *Guidepost* is a weekly aimed at the American community, while the *English Press* is English-language – but aimed at Spaniards.

Many big tourist centres have their own English-language sheet, with local events. *Look-out* magazine, based in Malaga, covers events right across Spain and also brings out some useful publications. Benidorm has the *Costa Blanca News* and in Barcelona the local monthly guide *Vivir en Barcelona* has an English section. In Palma de Mallorca the *Majorca Daily Bulletin* is published.

TV AND RADIO

After the British, the Spanish spend more time glued to their television sets than anyone else in Europe. There are televisions in homes where there are no fridges, even in the south. However there is unlikely to be one in a holiday let, unless it is a private apartment. You are most likely to come across TV sets in bars, where they are set up high for all to see. Here you may catch the weather forecasts (*el boletín meteorológico*). These are largely in diagrams and are easy to follow. The daily news broadcasts are at at 3 p.m. on TVE 1 and TVE 2 and at 8.30 p.m. on TVE 1. Most Spaniards are accustomed to get their news from TV, and TVE (the state service) gives a great deal of coverage to official statements and views.

Light entertainment takes up a much lower proportion of TV time than it does in Britain, for there are more documentaries and educational programmes. However, for those who just want to relax in front of the screen, TVE 1 and 2 run

British and American classics late at night. These are usually dubbed, but they also run the original soundtrack simultaneously on the radio.

The radio has four local networks on medium wave, but most people listen to FM, which has more stations. The Spanish classical station is Radio Nacional 2, 96.5 MHz in Madrid, while the Madrid pop station is Radio Ochenta, 89.0 MHz. It's worth giving local stations a go, for local colour, and for news of events. Even if you don't grasp the whole, you can then enquire further. The local station near my holiday home is Radio Malaga and it broadcasts music that seems more Arab than Western – and plays 'Ave Maria' every morning at 11.55, with 5 minutes prayer.

Some Spanish stations in tourist areas have short broadcasts in English. The BBC World Service can be picked up in Spain on the shortwave between 13m and 49m. This is a 24-hour service – use the lower registers at night. In some parts of Spain you may also be able to pick this up on medium wave – and Radio 2 as well.

HEALTH

This chapter deals with the minor but aggravating things that can go wrong health-wise when you're abroad. For more serious matters, see LOCAL SERVICES in this Chapter and EMERGENCIES (Chapter 12).

STOMACH UPSETS AND DIARRHOEA

Upset stomachs can be caused as much by too much sun, as by the food, although children tend to double their fruit intake – and adults their wine intake – abroad. A day indoors, largely asleep, often works wonders.

In the case of diarrhoea, it's important to drink plenty of fluid, as dehydration can set in very quickly in Spain's hot climate. This is especially important for small children, and if you have an electrolyte powder (such as Dioralyte) with you, make use of it. If a bout of diarrhoea lasts for more than 24 hours you should seek medical attention.

Kaolin tablets (*caolín*) are an excellent corrective for diarrhoea caused by excess fruit and wine. As soon as the worst is past, eat some solid bready food. Lomotil (which you will have to bring with you, for it is on prescription) is the best medicine for stomach upsets caused by bugs in the water or bad hygiene. Don't buy meat that has been displayed in the sun or in fly-infested areas.

If your stomach is sensitive, avoid anything with milk, cream, yoghurt or mayonnaise in it. A change of diet itself can cause problems. I have experienced problems returning to Britain, where the diet is much higher in dairy fats. (By the way, it is noticeable in Spain that the low dairy-fat diet means almost no plaque on teeth.)

KEEPING COOL

The evaporation of sweat from the skin is the body's way of cooling down. Drink plenty of liquids (preferably water) to prevent dehydration. Children may protest that they're not thirsty, but ensure they drink at regular intervals. Take a *siesta* in the hottest part of the day. Wait until the late afternoon to sight-see or go to the beach.

SUN

Don't imagine that you can emulate that wonderful olive or mahogany tan that Spanish people develop – unless your skin is fairly dark already. Being in the sun can make you feel wonderful, but over-doing it can cause permanent damage to your skin. Not only can you get nastily burned, but a link has now been established between sudden, intense exposure to sun and skin cancer. You're most at risk if you have fair or freckled skin which burns before it tans, or if you have fair hair or light-coloured eyes. Protect yourself by:

- choosing a sunscreen that protects against both UVA and UVB

- reapplying sunscreen at regular intervals (water and sweat will wash it away)
- using sunscreen on cloudy days; the sun is just as harmful through cloud
- gradually building up the amount of time you spend in the sun; never stay in the sun until your skin goes red
- avoid sunbathing in the middle of the day when the sun is at its strongest
- covering up when you're walking round in the sun
- wearing a good pair of sunglasses to protect your eyes.

For bad burns – on adults or children – when the skin peels and the flesh turns scarlet – visit the pharmacy for advice. You may be recommended lanolin (*lanolina*) to smooth thickly on the affected area. Keep covered up and try to keep in the shade as well. Swim with a shirt on until the burns have healed completely.

SUNSTROKE

This is accompanied by headache and sickness. A day in bed in a darkened room, drinking juice usually cures it. Broken veins in the eyes, making them look yellow, are one temporary but unpleasant form. Polarized sunglasses help to prevent this.

SALMONELLA

Be careful – hot weather makes bacteria breed at a fearful rate. Raw poultry is the main cause, through being put down on boards which are not then scrubbed before being used for something else, or by cooks using the same fork to poke or turn birds, and then to move other food. It is this sort of thing that transfers salmonella from raw poultry back to cooked poultry. If poultry is basted with marinade it must then be heated thoroughly again. Never serve poultry in the unwashed marinade bowl – although this seems natural when barbecuing in the garden.

CACTUSES

See under CHILDREN AND BABIES, Chapter 9.

STAYING SAFE

A few final tips to ensure that your holiday is happy and healthy.

- never let children in the water without at least one capable swimmer to keep an eye on them
- always check that the water is deep enough before diving
- stay away from animals that might bite or scratch – you risk catching rabies
- avoid riding motorbikes and bikes unless you have the right protective clothing
- make sure you know who to contact in an emergency. (See EMERGENCIES, Chapter 12.)

DRIVING

Cars are still registered by cities in Spain, showing where they come from. For example MA is from Malaga, SE from Seville. Locals often carry regional discs as well. For example a sign with red and yellow vertical stripes and a C is for Catalonia, while Galicia shows a G on a white background with a blue band. SEAT are the national car firm, making popular little models.

Driving in Spain is the single most likely area of friction between natives and foreigners.

ROADS

Toll routes (*los autopista peaje*) have an A prefix on road maps. Apart from a network round Madrid, there are two major ones. The first runs from Bilbao on the north coast to Barcelona on the east coast, crossing the country via Zaragossa. The second connects Spain to the French toll route along the Mediterranean shore, and so with the Toulouse, Entre Deux Mers toll route. This toll road runs from the eastern frontier as far as Alicante.

Los carreteras nacionales are a network radiating from Madrid, fast motorways outside the capital and straight too. Main roads have prefix CN or N on map. A big highway now connects Madrid straight through to Malaga on the south coast. The connection from Madrid to Bilbao is by no means as good.

However, geography is against the road builders in Europe's most mountainous country, where the peaks are second only to Switzerland in height. The central *meseta* may be flat, but elsewhere there is a good deal of roller-coaster driving, while the Santander coast road going west is one of worst major highways in Europe.

Many of the back roads are appalling. Heavy rain and snow take their toll every winter and parts slip away. Watch for emergency markers, showing that part of the road has fallen away, and also for boulders. You will also see stone huts labelled *peatones*, overnight refuges (before motor transport) for poor roadworkers on the repair job. Mountain passes may be shut in winter – and not only in the Pyrenees. A closure should be signalled by a board lower down the mountain. High roads have side posts to indicate the depth of standing snow.

HIGHWAY CODE *(Codigo de la circulation)*

On main highways the rule is to drive in the fast lane of dual carriageways. The slow lane is reserved for carts, tractors and slow vehicles. Up hills on major highways and motorways there will be an extra lane for these. The Spanish have a sensible system of looping off the road to the right, in order to make a left turn. An exit is a *cambio de sentido*.

Speed limits vary according to the type of road: 120km/h (74 mph) is allowed on motorways, 100km/h (62mph) on other main roads. On minor roads the maximum is 90km/h (56mph) and in built-up areas 60km/h (37mph). A car towing is limited to 80km/h (50mph).

A solid white line is the equivalent of our double line. No overtaking or turning left is allowed. The no-overtaking sign on roads is easy to recognize – a black car and a red car (or sometimes a lorry). The rule is to give way – *ceda el paseo* – to traffic from the right. Be particularly careful on big roundabouts in cities. *Macho* drivers have a nasty habit of joining the roundabout to your right, leaping for the central, priority, lane and then jumping off the roundabout ahead of you and to your left. Most off-putting the first time!

Traffic lights *(los semáforos)* pass straight from red to green, so an amber light automatically means slow down, red to follow. Overhead lights can be difficult to see against the sun, but there is an additional light low on the pole for those nearest to it.

Despacio means go slowly – often because of *obras*, road works. *Prohibito el paso* is no entry and *carretera cortado*, road partially blocked.

Since fewer people have cars, roads are much used for walking, especially near villages. People generally walk towards the oncoming traffic. Look out for them, as they carry no lights – and nor do donkeys, tractors and hay carts.

Wearing seat belts is compulsory outside towns and wherever you see the notices *uso obligatorio del cinturón de seguridad*. Lights should be dipped in towns.

Motoring in towns, especially in the old quarters, can be a hazardous business, with complicated one-way systems. It is easy to get stuck behind a stationary car, while the driver chats to passing friends, or behind one that remains driverless for 10 minutes.

PARKING *(aparcamiento)*

Prohibito aparcar and *estacionamiento prohibido* both mean No Parking. Don't park less than 5m (16ft) from a corner. Nor may you stop for more than 2 minutes on a solid yellow line, on zigzag yellow lines or on dotted lines. You may only stop in an emergency on the side of a motorway. Many towns also have odd and even dates parking on alternate sides of the street, marked by blue notices. There are also blue zones, where parking is not permitted between 8 a.m. and 9 p.m. for more than 1½ hours, and a parking disc must be obtained and displayed. This is one of the things to ask at any local tourist office: *¿Hace falta discos de aparcamiento aquí?*

In cities like Barcelona in the evening there are cars cruising all the time, looking for parking, and hovering round existing parks, waiting for departures. Apart from modern purpose-built car parks in big cities, you will also find *estacionamento reglamentados* car parks in city squares with a guardian. Ask: Can I park here: *¿Se puede parcar aquí?* The ticket fee will be small. If the man helps you with your shopping it is usual to give him another small coin too.

POLICE AND INSTANT FINES *(Policia y las multas)*

Apart from radar speed traps, the police run drug checks,

stopping lines of cars, particularly on the major roads in the south. Since many foreign criminals have found haven in Spain, having a foreign licence plate does not make it more likely that your car will be waved through. On this type of check they may well run an eye over your papers, driving licence (*permiso de conducir*), green card, ownership certificate, all of which must be carried at all times by law.

Offences are *infracciones* and on-the-spot fines (*las multas*) apply in Spain (up to £150). The legal limit for drinking and driving is 0.8g alcohol per 1000cc.

The Guarda Civil patrol in pairs on motorbikes, waiting at spots like tunnel exits for cars exceeding speed limits. And they are not likely to let you off on the grounds of being an ignorant foreigner. If you are very lucky, the local police might be more lenient and overlook a parking offence, provided you don't rub them up the wrong way.

PETROL STATIONS (*gasolineras*)

Spain is a large country and while villages of medium size have petrol stations, smaller ones well may not. Start thinking about a refill when your tank is still a quarter full if you are not in familiar territory.

Estaciones de servicio are service stations open from about 7 a.m. till about 10 p.m. There are a few 24-hour garages. They sell four grades of petrol (*gasolina*) and now that Britain has litres too, you'll not find working out the prices a problem. Ninety-octane is called *normal*, 96 (*super*) is nearest to our 4-star, 98 is *extra*. Unleaded petrol (*gasolina sin plombo*) is by no means common. Diesel is *gasóleo*, while you'll have no difficulty in buying the international brands of oil.

Rigged pumps used to be common some years ago – they showed more fuel had passed into your tank than was the case. If this happens to you, next time go to a CAMPSA, a filling station which is part government owned. Prices here are standardized all over the country.

Middle-class Spaniards don't like getting their hands dirty, so attendants are accustomed to do extra jobs like checking the tyres (*la presíon de los neumáticos*) and expect a coin in return.

As in other countries, garages in Spain offer services like toilets. Ask: *¿Hay servicios?* They also sell bags of ice cubes (*cubitos de hielo*).

USEFUL PHRASES

Put in 20 litres: *Déme veinte litros* (or just *arriba*: full up).
Please check the oil (water): *Por favor, controle la aceite (agua)*.
Would you clean the windscreen: *Quiere limpiar el parabrisas*.

BREAKDOWN AND CAR REPAIRS

The Spanish have a good reputation as ingenious mechanics, so can probably get you out of a fix even if you run into trouble far from a garage specializing in your make of vehicle. They will repair and make do in a clever fashion, even when the exact part is not available.

Spanish mechanics also work extremely long hours, and it is even possible to find a garage open at Saturday teatime. And labour costs are lower here than in other European countries.

Spare parts are available through garages which are authorized agents, and it might be a good idea to take along a list of these from home if your car is unusual.

USEFUL PHRASES

Where's the nearest garage?: *¿Dónde está el garage más cercano?* I've broken down: *Tengo un coche estropeado*.
I have a puncture: *Tengo un pinchazo*.
There's something wrong with the brakes (clutch, accelerator): *Le pasa algo con el freno (embrague, acelerador)*.
How long will you be?: *¿Cuánto tardarán?*
Car is *un coche*.

CONTACT WITH HOME

POST *(el correo)*

Post offices *(oficinas de correos)* are open Monday to Friday from 9 a.m. to 2 p.m. then from 5 p.m. to 7.30 p.m., and on Saturday from 9 a.m. to 1 p.m. although you cannot send a parcel on Saturday. Stamps *(sellos)* are widely sold in tobacconists *(estanco)*, and many postcard shops and hotels sell them too. Post boxes are yellow; put letters home in the opening marked *extranjero*. Post from Spain is reliable and reasonably quick, taking about five days.

RECEIVING MAIL IN SPAIN

Even though you have a full address, it does not follow that letters can be delivered there. In towns many apartment blocks have a mail delivery, but houses outside towns may not have the same service. If you are renting someone else's home they probably pay for a mail box, a litle steel-doored cubby hole at the post office. A key for this should be part of the keys to your apartment. Go along with the key and inspect the contents.

SPANISH ADDRESSES

The address system reflects the fact that most people in Spain live in apartments. The name of the street may be followed by a series of numbers: the first is the number in the street (the apartment block), the second is the storey *(piso)*, usually reduced to ° after the number, and the third is the door number *(puerta)* with a tiny, raised *a*. 'Care of' in Spanish is *c/de*.

POSTE RESTANTE

Every post office operates a *poste restante* service, free of charge. Tell people to write to: your name, *la lista de correos*, then the town and district in Spain – and also to put their own name and address on the outside of the letter and package.

A word of warning. Post to Spain is often very slow. This is a relic from the days of Franco and a suspicious, police-oriented bureaucracy. Letters still may go round via Madrid. With luck, letters can take a week from Britain, but two months is not extraordinary. If the letter is important – like money orders – don't rely on the post. It is also not worth asking someone to post a left-behind bikini top or bottom. You might never see it again!

TELEPHONE *(el teléfono)*

Automatic international calls *(conferencias internationales)* are possible from most telephone boxes. Ask: Is there a call box? *¿Hay un cabina de teléfono aquí?*

For an international call you will need a pile of 100 peseta coins. Rest the first one in the groove at the top, it falls when someone answers. To get a line, dial 07. A high monotone indicates you have an international line. Then dial 44 (for Britain) or 353 (for Eire), then the full number. Most area codes in Britain start with 0 inside the country. Drop this when you are ringing from abroad.

Foreigners are confused by phone boxes (and sometimes phones in bars too) that only permit local calls. If you find that you cannot get through to the international line say: I need to make a call on an outside line: *Quiero un conferencia urbana*. In a tourist centre, the boxes might be marked *conferencias urbanas* or *teléfonos internacionales*.

Spain also has telephone offices, the CTNE, known as *el Teléfonica*. In large towns these are open 24 hours a day. Ask: *¿Hay un Teléfonica aquí?* Here you can make your call first, and pay afterwards, which avoids the change problem. In some tourist areas there are also booths, with *teléfonos* on a green background, where an operator will make the connection for you and you can pay afterwards. (I want to pay for the call: *Queiro pagar la llamada*.) You can use hotels, but you'll be charged about 25% for the privilege.

If you want to reverse the charges, tell the operator – many international operators speak English. There are two codes to get the international operator, depending where in Spain you are ringing from. If you are in Madrid, dial 008. If you are in any other part of Spain, dial 9198.

Ask for *un conferencia a cobre revertido*. She will probably call you back, so check your postbox number, plus the Spanish provincial code. This will start with 9 and should be written up in the box, although not on the phone itself. Remember that Spain is one hour in advance of Britain in summer, although the EEC is trying to standardize summer time.

If your rented appartment has a phone, people can phone you there more cheaply than you can phone them. The code from Britain is 010 34, then the regional and local code.

CHAPTER TWELVE

EMERGENCIES

EMERGENCY TELEPHONE

For emergencies of the fire/police/ambulance variety, dial 091. There is no central emergency number, as we have, but in large towns emergency calls go straight through to the police. Local phone booths and local newspapapers may list other local numbers.

If there is a serious accident, ask for *un equipo quirúrgico* (surgical team). Ambulances (*ambulancias*) exist but there are fewer of them proportionately. The Spanish system is to stop the first car and ask the driver (technically he ought not to refuse) to drive you to the nearest hospital. While someone waves a white hanky out of the window he can then rush you there, ignoring traffic signs, while other cars should give way. Don't try this as a joke. There is a heavy fine if caught.

USEFUL PHRASES

Where is the nearest telephone: *¿Donde esta el teléfono más cerca de aquí?*

There are people hurt: *Hay gente herida.*

Call a doctor: *Llama un medico.*

Casas de Socorros are emergency units in various parts of towns, where first aid is available. The Red Cross (*Cruz Rojo*) runs the first aid stations (*Puestos de Socorro*) on some roads.

HOSPITAL, DOCTOR AND DENTIST

Locate a doctor (*un medico*) by asking your caretaker, a pharmacist or, if all else fails, in the nearest bar. The ratio of doctors to inhabitants in Spain is well up to West European standards and they are very good. However, some British residents suggest you avoid the dentists unless it's a real emergency. There are two types of hospital – private and social security. The reciprocal EC arrangement (for which you need a Form E111) entitles you to social security treatment only, whereas travel insurance enables you to use the private system. In either case you may be expected to pay up front and reclaim from insurance when you get home. There is more information about doctors, payment and insurance in Chapter 4, GETTING READY.

POLICE

There are two types of police that you are likely to encounter. The *policia municipal*, recognizable by their blue shirts, are recruited locally and their job is to enforce local bylaws, chiefly controlling traffic in towns. Nevertheless they wear guns and carry batons. They run the local police stations (*comisaria*) where you should take complaints about lost property (see below).

The *guardia civil* are distinguished by green uniforms and once wore black patent-leather hats with flattened wings at the back, under which their dark spectacles always looked sinister. They are the military police, and under Franco they were always stationed in areas away from their homes, so that they were not susceptible to local influence. They form the highway patrols, often riding as a pair on motorbikes, colloquially known as *la pareja* (the couple). They also patrol in landrovers and one of their jobs is to enforce speed limits. They are a very professional force and in an emergency they can be extremely helpful. In parts of the country, particularly on the south coast road around Malaga they run traffic blocks, stopping vehicles to search for drugs. The British are apparently now a major criminal element on the south coast and the police believe they are entitled at least to enquire whether you are connected to one of these criminal groups. Spain has also put up with a lot of football hooliganism.

It is worth bearing in mind that these are the same personnel as served under Franco, and that the older ones will have had their training in that era.

There is also a third, brown-shirted police force, the *policia nacional*, who guard installations and do some patrolling.

LOST PROPERTY AND THEFT
(objetos perdidos e robo)

Generally there is more crime against property than against the person in Spain. Bag snatching by passing motorbikers is common in cities in Spain. Wear your camera or shoulderbag on the side away from the street. Lock your car whenever you leave it, even if for only a short time. *Never* leave valuables or other property in the car. If this is unavoidable, hide things under rugs so that they are not visible. Keep the record of the numbers of your travellers cheques in a different pocket or part of the car.

Townhalls run lost property offices (*oficina de objetos perdidos*). Even if your handbag is stolen, you may get your passport and some papers back, even though the money has gone. Unsaleable items may be put into local postboxes and then circulate through to the police or lost property. You will need something to identity yourself when claiming them.

When reporting any theft or loss, always take your passport with you, otherwise the police won't do anything. If you lose your passport, report it to the local British consul – replacement will be easier if you have a photocopy of it.

CONSULAR SERVICES *(consulate)*

Don't approach the local British consul *(cónsul)* for services that would be provided by the police or local hospital at home. It's not their job – nor have they power – to skip over local regulations and get you a special service. But they are always there if you have your back to the wall. For example, a lost passport – needed in Spain to change money – and in particular to get back into Britain without passing through a detention centre; destitution – no money, cards, contacts or prospects; no means of getting home – particularly for the under 16s; and general catastrophe. But not the mishaps of the holiday that turns out to be a nightmare, because of a score of small things that just go wrong.

INSURANCE

As a general rule, make sure you take your insurance policy with you and any emergency telephone numbers they supply you with. If you are going to make any sort of claim, keep all receipts, etc., carefully, and (in the case of theft or loss) make sure that you have made a report to the police or your claim may be void.

LOST CREDIT CARDS

The minute you discover your credit card is missing, phone the 24-hour 'Lost and stolen' number. Report it at home, not in Spain (apart from American Express, see below).

The 'Lost and stolen' numbers for the UK are:

- VISA 07 (wait for high tone) 44 604 230230
- ACCESS 07 (wait for high tone) 44 702 362988
- AMERICAN EXPRESS 07 (wait for high tone) 44 273 696933 (or contact any local American Express office)

If you have no cash dial the operator and ask for a reverse charge call (see Chapter 11, CONTACT WITH HOME). The credit card company will accept the call.

LOST TRAVELLERS CHEQUES

When you get travellers cheques you get a record sheet and instructions about what to do in case of loss or theft – it really is wise to hang on to these and keep them safe. You must keep a record of the cheque numbers, and of ones that are used so that you know exactly which ones are lost. If not, a lost cheque is like a lost banknote – gone, irreplaceable.

You will have been given a form with instructions about what to do in case of loss. For American Express, contact the nearest office, and the cheques will be replaced after much form-filling. If your travellers cheques are from a bank or building society and you don't have the instructions about what to do, go to a Spanish bank, or a branch of any UK bank and they may be able to put you on the right track. The tourist office in a large centre may also have some useful addresses. You can also use the international directory enquiries to find out the number of your bank at home and phone direct.

CHAPTER THIRTEEN

BUYING THINGS TO TAKE HOME

Spain has such a wealth of different products that you should be able to find something in the souvenir line to please either yourselves or your friends and relatives. Since this is a self-catering book, we have assumed that you might want to continue to enjoy some of the culinary discoveries once you get back home, and have included a section on eatables that you can (and can't) bring back.

When considering what to buy, give some thought to whether you will really want it by the time you get home. That delectable liqueur may not taste the same as it did when sipped under the Spanish moon, and that irresistible rug may not in fact go with anything else in the house.

FOOD AND DRINK

'Pure' olive oil, for me, is a must, for cooking and mayonnaise. The price per litre in Spain is what you pay for a pint in Britain. I buy 5-litre containers of some big brand like Covadonga.

Sadly it is not legal to bring any type of meat from any European country unless it is hermetically sealed. Obeying this restriction cuts out raw hams and *salchichones*. However, you may be able to find sealed packets in *hipermercados*. Cured fish like *mojama* and fish *salones* are allowed, as are any sort of can, like L'Escala *anchoas* – the best canned anchovies.

Sugared almonds *almendras garapiñadas* are good. Another

217

luxurious preserve is *marrons glacés*. Made in the north, these crystallized chestnuts are known by the French name, but they are smaller and sweeter than the French ones and amazingly sugary. The muscatel raisins (*pasas*) of Malaga are also outstanding, while prunes (*pasas de ciruelas*) are delicious if soaked in part of your holiday ration of *anís*.

Reserva Riojas can be bought in London for a fiver upwards, so it's hardly worth struggling with the weight to save a couple of pounds. So for red, at least, I would look at *Gran Reservas*. Anything with *Marqués* on it, white or red, will be a good buy, as will any Torres wine with *Gran* as part of its title. Don't buy anything over 10 years old, unless you are knowledgeable about wine (note: 1984 and 1985 were the two bad years of the decade).

When you get the wine home, don't shove the bottles into the back of the cupboard and leave them, hoping they will get better. They won't. Spanish wines, unlike many French ones, are matured by the *bodega* and only put on the market when ready to drink.

Basic brandy, like Fundador which flames well, is a good buy for Christmas. The better ones, such as Carlos I, II and III, are as good as French cognac and much cheaper. The international liqueurs like Cointreau are also much cheaper in Spain. If you want a local orange liqueur, try Mascaró.

UK CUSTOMS ALLOWANCE

The first thing to grasp is that your allowance is larger if bought outside a duty free shop, because it has paid tax in the country of origin. Duty-frees are mainly for travellers by air and ship. As well as spirits and wine there is a third customs category which includes fortified wines, sparkling wine and liqueurs under 22%.

If you are travelling by car, and want to carry your entire allowance in still wine, two people are allowed 16 litres together, that is 21 bottles of 75ml size, if bought in Spanish shops. You can't then take any other duty-free alcohol.

ALLOWANCES BOUGHT FROM DUTY-FREE SHOPS

- 1 litre spirits, liqueurs etc. over 22%

  or

  2 litres not over 22% (sherry, sparkling wine)

  plus

  2 litres still wine

  OR
- 4 litres of wine only

ALLOWANCES BOUGHT FROM SPANISH SHOPS

- 1.5 litres spirits, liqueurs etc. over 22%

  or

  3 litres not over 22%

  plus

  5 litres still wine

  OR
- 8 litres of wine only

KITCHEN THINGS

Ceramics are pretty in Spain, particularly when painted in Arab colours of turquoise and blue. A big platter for arranged salads or fruit will cost half the UK price. A big fruit bowl, with a set of individual bowls might also be useful, although Spanish painted earthenware chips far more easily than our fired china.

Brown oven dishes (*cazuelas*) come in a variety of qualities from very crude and cheap to sophisticated. A set of little oven dishes will be a fraction of the French price. Spaniards also like glass plates and a glass platter may be a good buy.

Pots and pans are cheap, so if you have a car to carry them home, this is an opportunity to acquire big ones. A *paella* pan will show off your acquired Spanish cooking. A true *paella* pan for rice has a dimpled bottom so that the rice does not catch. For general use I would choose one 30cm/12in diameter with 5cm/2in-high sides, large enough for a splendid party *paella* for 6 or even 8 people.

If you have often thought vaguely at home about buying a

big stock pot, now's your chance. A huge Spanish enamelled casserole of the 14-litre sort is half the price of a 3-gallon aluminium stock pot, and a quarter the price of stainless steel pans of the same size in Britain.

CLOTHING, JEWELLERY AND PERFUME

Spain has become a serious contributor to the international fashion and design market in recent years. There is now a wide range of stylish clothing from designers in Madrid and Barcelona.

Leather clothes, bags, shoes and other accessories are all worth considering if you want something with a bit of extra flair and style. Ibiza is the centre of high fashion, and you can get things there (at a price) that you won't find on the mainland. Clothing is expensive, it must be said, so unless you're a serious dresser, you may not find it worth the outlay. Leather bags and shoes are about the same price as in the UK, but the quality is better. The Spanish export their lower quality stuff! Hats can be interesting too, if they're part of local dress, and they won't be too expensive.

Spanish babies' and children's clothes can be beautiful, and there is often a much larger range than in Britain – so if you have children, or are looking for gifts, you could visit one of the specialist children's boutiques or section of a department store. Little girls who like dressing up for parties might like the full-skirted flamenco outfits that you can buy.

Costume jewellery and traditional gold and silver jewellery are both widely available, in both shops and markets. The famous Majorica pearls from Mallorca are worth buying, if your taste lies in that direction, because although they are cultured pearls, they are very good ones.

Perfume (from the *perfumería* or department stores) and cosmetics are generally much cheaper in Spain – even the familiar brands, which can be half the UK price, and also cheaper than the duty free shop.

CRAFTS

There are still numerous small craft workers all over Spain, making goods in the time-honoured way, and the quality can be very good indeed. In Mallorca, for example, the leatherwork is of very high quality, the prices will be comparable with the UK. Pottery – both for the kitchen and ornamental – can be found in most regions, and also ceramics – which still retain their regional variations and make good presents.

If you have room to carry them you might want to consider beaten copper work (Granada, Guadalupe), wrought iron (Seville), ceramics (Aragon, Balearic Islands, Castile) and pottery (Catalonia). Lladro pottery is popular – if you can carry it – and is half the UK price.

Lace work is of high quality, and lace table linen can be particularly good value. If you're in a small village where the older people still make lace items, you can pick up a very good bargain still. The same goes for knitwear – the local wool shop sometimes has high-quality hand-knitted items made by local people. Spanish fans are the quintessential reminder of Spain, and some of them are hand-painted and make good decorative items – they are also highly practical in the southern heat.

However, you needn't necessarily go to an area to buy its products, there are chain shops such as Gallerias, Artespaña and El Corte Inglés, that sell a vast range of goods, including arts and crafts from all over Spain. If you have a hypermarket near you, you'll find that it probably has a good section of gifts and souvenirs too.

The Spanish go in for British pop music in a big way, but the prices of records and tapes will be higher than in the UK. However, if you hear locally produced Spanish music that you like, for example the Gypsy Kings or flamenco music, why not try buying records or tapes in Spain.

Index

ABTA, 29
accidents, 212
accommodation, 15–22
  booking, 25–37
  caretakers, 71–3
  inventories, 19,
    66–71
address system, 209
advertisements, 25–7
air-conditioning, 21
AITO, 30
alcohol, 75, 77, 78–86,
  124, 207, 218–19
ambulances, 212
Andalucia, 12–13
ants, 183, 188
apartment blocks, 15, 16
aperitifs, 79
apples, 112, 158
artichokes, 110, 135,
  147–8
asparagus, 138–9
Asturias, 10–11
ATOL, 29–30
aubergines, 109, 170–1,
  177
avocados, 145–6

babies *see* children
babysitters, 184–5
Bail Bonds, 60
banks, 55, 195
barbecues, 172–7
Barcelona, 13, 87–90
bars, 87
Basque country, 11
bathrooms, 21
BBC World Service, 200
beaches, 181–2
bedrooms, 21
beer, 78
bidets, 21, 189–90
bills, restaurants, 98
birds, eating, 96,
  114–15
blocked drains, 189–90

boats, documents, 59
bocadillos, 126–9
bodegas, 87
booking
  accommodation,
    25–37
brandy, 84–5, 218
bread, 100, 102–3,
  126–9
breakdowns, cars, 208
breakfast, 75, 178
buses, 195–6
butane gas ovens, 21–2,
  187
butchers, 100, 115
butter, 106

cactuses, 113, 183–4
cafes, 87
cake shops, 90
cakes, 98, 103–4
cancellations, 26
caretakers, 71–3
cars: children in, 23–4
  documents, 58–9
  driving, 204–8
  equipment, 60–1
  hiring, 47–8
  insurance, 54, 59–60
  travelling to Spain,
    23–4, 38–41
cash, 55–6
cash dispensers, 57
ceramics, 219, 221
cesspits, 181, 187
charcuterie, 115–18
charge cards, 57–8
cheese, 107–8, 144, 158
chicken, 96, 114, 142–3,
  149, 202
chickpeas, 172–5
children: baby food and
  equipment, 180
  clothing, 220
  food, 178–9
  medical care, 183,

  200–1
  passports, 51
  safety, 181–4
  travelling, 23–4, 46
chocolate, 105, 178
cider, 78–79
clams, 162
clothing, 220
cod, salt, 106
coffee, 77, 86, 105
complaints, in
  restaurants, 98
consular services, 215
Costa Almeria, 13
Costa Blanca, 13
Costa Brava, 13–14
Costa Calida, 13
Costa de la Luz, 12
Costa del Azahar, 13
Costa del Sol, 12–13
Costa Dorada, 13
Costa Vasca, 11
Costa Verde, 11
costs, 19–20
cots, 21
crafts, 221
cream cheese, 115, 143
credit cards, 52, 55,
  57–8, 215–16
crime, 214
custard apples, 169
customs allowances,
  218–19

dehydration, 200–1
dentists, 61, 213
deposits, 26
dessert wines, 83–4, 146
desserts, 97–8
diarrhoea, 200–1
doctors, 213
donkeys, 197–8
drains, blocked, 189–90
drinking water, 76–7, 78
drinks, 77–86, 124,
  218–19

driving *see* cars
driving licences, 58–9
dry cleaning, 189
duty-free allowances, 218–19

E111 form, 52–3
eating out, 86–98
eggs, 93–4, 108, 133–4, 165–6
electricity, 22, 186
emergencies, 212–16
Eurocheques, 55, 57
Extremadura, 12
ferries, 38, 41–4
figs, 113, 147
fines, driving offences, 207
fire, emergencies, 212
first aid kits, 61–2
fish, 95–6, 100, 118–20, 217
    recipes, 136–7, 145–6, 150–2, 164–8, 175–6
flats, 16
flying to Spain, 38, 45–7
food: eating out, 86–98
    menus and recipes, 125–79
    shopping, 99–124
    souvenirs, 217–18
food poisoning, 202
fortified wines, 84
fruit, 112–16
fuses, 186

Galicia, 10
game, 96, 114–15
garages, 207–8
gas, butane ovens, 21–2, 187
Granada, 12
grapes, 113, 152
Green Cards, 59–60
grey mullet, 166–8
groceries, 105–6

hairdressers, 198
ham, raw, 117, 150

hayfever, 62
headlights, 60
health care *see* medical care
heat stroke, 202
herbs, 111–12
hiring: cars, 47–8
    velos (mopeds), 197
holidays, public, 101–2
home exchanges, 27
hospitals, 213
housekeeping, 186–92
hovercraft, 38, 42

Ibiza, 14
ice cream, 97–8, 107, 146
inns, 87
insects, 183, 188
insurance, 215
    cars, 59–60
    medical, 213
    travel, 26, 51–2, 54
inventories, 19, 66–71

jam, 105
jewellery, 220
junket, 107, 143

kebabs, 129
kidneys, recipes, 160–3
kitchens, 21–2
    equipment, 22, 219–20

laundry, 189
lavatories, 180–1, 187
leather goods, 220, 221
lemons, 112
Leon, 12
lifestyle, 75–6
light meals, 126–79
lighting, 21
liqueurs, 85–6, 218
loquats, 113
lost property, 214
luggage, 47, 63–7
lunch, 75

Madrid, 11–12, 87–90
magazines, 198–9
mail boxes, 209
Mallorca, 14
La Mancha, 12
markets, 99–100
measurements, 126
meat, 96–7, 115–18, 217
medical care: ailments, 61–2, 200–2
    emergencies, 213
    first aid, 61–2
    Form E111, 52–3
    pharmacies, 193–4
melons, 112–15, 150
Menorca, 14
menus, 92–8, 125–79
merenderos (cafes), 87
milk, 107
money, 55–8, 195
mopeds, 197
mosquitoes, 183, 189
Motorail, 38, 40–1
motorways, 204
mountain passes and tunnels, 48, 205
mullet, 145–6, 166–8
muscatel grapes, 113, 146
mushrooms, 110, 169
music, 221
mussels, 157–8

nappies, 181, 183
Navarra, 11
newspapers, 198–9

Old Castile, 12
olive oil, 105–6, 217
olives, 105
omelettes, 133–4
opening hours, 101–2
oranges, 112, 134, 177
ovens, butane gas, 21–2, 187

packing, 63–7
paella, 150–2, 219
paradors (hotels), 87
parking, 206

passes, mountain, 48, 205
passports, 51, 214, 215
pasta, 94, 105
pears, 112, 162
peppers, 109, 128, 132, 164–5
perfume, 220
persimmons, 113
petrol, 207–8
pharmacies, 193–4
police, 206–7, 213–14
pomegranates, 113
pork, 129, 154–5, 163
post restante, 209–10
postal services, 209–10
potatoes, 109–10, 156–7, 163
pottery, 219, 221
poultry, 96, 114–15, 202
prawns, 130
prickly pears, 113
pueblos, 16–19
punches, 86
Pyrenees, 14

rabies, 203
radios, 200
railways, 38, 40–1, 44–5, 196
raisins, 146
rating system, rented apartments, 19
recipes, 125–79
red mullet, 145–6
refrescos (soft drinks), 78
restaurants, 75–6, 86–90, 92–8, 178, 179
rice, 94, 105, 150–2, 154–5
roads, 204–6

rubbish, 188–9

Saints days, 101–2
salads, 92, 110–11, 127–8 131–2, 144–6, 153, 164–5, 172–5, 177
salmonella, 202
salt cod, 106
San Sebastian, 87–90
sandwiches, 126–9
sausages, 116–17
Seacat, 43
seat belts, 206
Seville, 12
shellfish, 95, 120–4, 150–2
sherry, 79–80, 218
shopping, 73–4, 99–124, 180, 193–4
sinks, blocked, 190
snacks, 76, 179
soft drinks, 78
soups, 93, 157–8
souvenirs, 217–21
sparkling wines, 83
speed limits, 205, 207
spices, 106
spinach, 110, 159–60
starters, 92
stomach upsets, 200–1
sunburn, 182, 201–2
supermarkets, 100, 101, 193
supper, 75
sweet breads, 103
sweets, 101, 103

tabernas (bars), 87
tapas (snacks), 90–2, 179

tascas (bars), 87
taxis, 197
tea, 77, 105
telephone books, 190, 198
telephones, 60, 198, 210–11, 212
television, 199–200
theft, 214
time zones, 211
tipping, 98, 197, 198
toilets, 180–1, 187
toll roads, 204
tomatoes, 109, 127, 144, 147–8, 156–7, 177
tortilla (omelettes), 93, 133
traffic lights, 205
trains, 38, 40–1, 44–5, 196
travel companies, 27–8
travel: to Spain, 38–50 in Spain, 195–8 *see also* cars
travellers cheques, 55, 56, 214, 216
tuna, 164–5, 175–6
tunnels, 48

urbanizaciones, 15–16

Valencia, 13
vegetables, 94–5, 109–11
velos (mopeds), 197
villas, 16
vinegar, 106

water, 76–7, 78, 187
wine, 80–4, 124, 218–19

Yellow Pages, 190, 198